MARTINI MADNESS

380 recipes to tempt your taste buds

DAVE A VANCE

This book contains adult language and is only suitable for adults of legal drinking age.

ISBN-13: 978-1-441455-55-0
ISBN-10: 1-441455-55-8

CONTENTS

PREFACE

The martini, once thought of as an old drink with gin, vermouth and olives has come a long way. Martinis now are made in any number of flavors with an ever increasing list of ingredients. If the classic martini doesn't interest you, try a fruit flavored martini, such as watermelon, apple, orange, banana or kiwi. If you're looking for a completely unique martini flavor, try a chocolate mint or double fudge martini. These are only examples of some of the martini flavors you will find in this book. The martini is no longer a drink ordered by a select few bar patrons. Martinis are hot sellers and make up a large portion of bar sales each year. Martini drinkers are abundant enough where bars and clubs are designing specialty martinis exclusive to their establishment.

The purpose of Martini Madness is to provide a wide variety of martini recipes. The only perfect martini is the martini that suits your palette, so I encourage you to experiment with techniques and flavors to find your perfect martini. I also encourage bar and club owners to create their own signature martinis to distinguish them from every other competitor. After all, making a martini is more of an art than just throwing ingredients together.

The recipes have been broken into sections, such as Gin, Vodka, Rum, Scotch, Tequila, Whiskey/Bourbon and Other. While a recipe may contain multiple ingredients from each of these types of liquor, I have broken them into the categories based on their base ingredient. On a limited basis, I have placed a few recipes in multiple categories.

While I do drink flavored martinis, my preference is the classic dirty martini. Instead of using vermouth as an actual ingredient, I swirl a dash or two of the vermouth in a chilled martini glass and pour it out before straining my drink into the glass. I don't care much for vermouth, but coating the inside of the glass gives my martini the perfect flavor. Remember, the perfect martini is the martini that tastes great to you, so you may find that this technique doesn't suit your taste.

If you want to know about the history of the martini and the many stories of its origin, I recommend searching the Internet for "The History of the Martini" in your favorite search engine.

CHILLING THE MARTINI GLASS

Serving a martini in a chilled glass is just as important as mixing the ingredients. A martini is typically not a drink that is served at room temperature or warm. Failing to chill a martini glass can result in a mediocre tasting martini or can even cause the martini to be downright undrinkable.

If available, rinse a martini glass and place it into a freezer for approximately ten minutes. Do not dry the glass after rinsing, as it will chill faster when wet.

If you do not have the time to pre-chill a martini glass in a freezer, you can use the quick and effective method of using water and ice. Rinse a martini glass with water to remove any dust or dirt and fill completely with crushed ice and water. Allow the glass to chill while you're making the martini. Three to four minutes should suffice, but the longer you leave it, the colder the glass will become. Once chilled, pour the ice and water out. You are now ready to pour your martini into the glass.

GIN

MARTINIS

Absinthe Martini

2 oz. Gin
1/2 oz. Dry Vermouth
1/8 tsp. Absinthe Herbal
   Liqueur
1 Onion Stuffed Olive

Combine ingredients in a mixing glass with cracked ice. Stir well and strain into a chilled martini glass. Garnish with an onion stuffed olive.

Angel's Breast Martini

2 oz. Gin
1 oz. White Creme de Cacao
1 oz. Godiva White
   Chocolate Liqueur
1 oz. Light Cream

Combine ingredients in a mixing glass with cracked ice. Shake and strain into a chilled martini glass.

Aperitivo Martini

6 parts Gin
3 parts White Sambuca
3 to 5 dashes Orange Bitters
1 Orange Peel

Combine liquid ingredients in a mixing glass with cracked ice. Stir to chill and strain into a chilled martini glass. Garnish with an orange peel.

Apollo Martini

2 1/2 oz. Gin
1 oz. White Creme de Cacao
1/2 oz. Blue Curacao

Combine ingredients in a mixing glass with cracked ice. Stir to chill and strain into a chilled martini glass.

Apricot-Mango Martini

2 pieces Fresh Mangos
2 1/2 oz. Tanqueray Gin
1/2 oz. Apricot Brandy
1/2 oz. Simple Syrup
1/2 oz. Fresh Lemon Juice
1 Twist Lemon Peel

Muddle fresh mango in the bottom of a mixing glass and add remaining ingredients with cracked ice. Shake well and strain into a chilled martini glass. Garnish with a twist of lemon peel.

Artillery Martini

6 parts Gin
2 parts Sweet Vermouth

Combine ingredients in a cocktail shaker with cracked ice. Shake well and strain into a chilled martini glass.

Ascot Martini

2 1/2 oz. Gin
1/2 oz. Sweet Vermouth
2 dashes Angostura Bitters

Combine ingredients in a mixing glass with cracked ice. Stir to chill and strain into a chilled martini glass.

Astor Place Martini

2 1/2 oz. Gin
1/2 oz. Galliano
1 dash Bitters

Combine ingredients in mixing glass with cracked ice. Stir to chill and strain into a chilled martini glass.

Astoria Martini

2 oz. Gin
1 oz. White Creme de Cacao
1 oz. Light Cream

Combine ingredients in a mixing glass with cracked ice. Shake and strain into a chilled martini glass.

Athena Martini

2 oz. Gin
1 oz. White Creme de Cacao
1 oz. Light Cream

Combine ingredients in a mixing glass with cracked ice. Shake and strain into a chilled martini glass.

Avenue B Martini

2 oz. Gin
1 oz. White Creme de Cacao
1/2 oz. Drambuie

Combine ingredients in mixing glass with cracked ice. Stir to chill and strain into a chilled martini glass.

Barnum Martini

6 parts Gin
1 part Apricot Brandy
3 to 5 dashes Angostura
    Bitters
3 to 5 dashes Lemon Juice

Combine ingredients in a cocktail shaker with cracked ice. Shake well and strain into a chilled martini glass.

Bee Line Martini

2 oz. Gin
1/2 oz. Peach Schnapps
1/2 oz. Apricot Brandy

Combine ingredients in mixing glass with cracked ice. Stir to chill and strain into a chilled martini glass.

Bennett Martini

6 parts Gin
1/2 tsp. Bar Sugar
3 to 5 dashes Angostura
  Bitters

Combine ingredients in a cocktail shaker with cracked ice. Shake well and strain into a chilled martini glass.

Black Martini

2/3 oz. Gin
1/3 oz. Black Sambuca

Combine ingredients in a cocktail shaker with cracked ice. Shake gently and strain into a chilled martini glass.

Bloodhound Martini

6 parts Gin
2 parts Sweet Vermouth
2 parts Dry Vermouth
3 Fresh Strawberries, hulled
1 Fresh Strawberry

Combine gin, sweet vermouth, dry vermouth and three fresh strawberries into a blender. Mix until well blended and pour into a chilled martini glass. Garnish with a fresh strawberry.

Blue Moon Martini

1 1/2 oz. Bombay Sapphire
  Gin
3/4 oz. Blue Curacao
  Liqueur
1 Lemon Twist

Combine liquid ingredients
in a mixing glass with
cracked ice. Stir well and
strain into a chilled martini
glass. Garnish with a lemon
twist.

Boomerang Martini

6 parts Gin
1 dash Angostura Bitters
2 parts Dry Vermouth
1 dash Maraschino Liqueur
1 Kiwi Slice

Combine liquid ingredients
in a mixing glass with
cracked ice. Stir to chill and
strain into a chilled martini
glass. Garnish with a kiwi
slice.

Braveheart Martini

2 1/2 oz. Gordon's London
  Dry Gin
1 tsp. Glenfiddich Scotch
1 Lemon Twist

Combine liquid ingredients
in a mixing glass with
cracked ice. Stir to chill and
strain into a chilled martini
glass. Garnish with a lemon
twist.

Broadway Martini

6 parts Gin
1 part White Creme de
  Menthe
1 Fresh Mint Sprig

Combine liquid ingredients
in a cocktail shaker with
cracked ice. Shake well and
strain into a chilled martini
glass. Garnish with a mint
sprig.

Bronx Tale Martini

2 oz. Gin
1 oz. Orange Juice
1 tsp. Dry Vermouth

Combine ingredients in a cocktail shaker with cracked ice. Shake and strain into a chilled martini glass.

Bronx Terrace Martini

6 parts Gin
2 parts Fresh Lime Juice
1 part Dry Vermouth
1 Maraschino Cherry

Combine liquid ingredients in a cocktail shaker with cracked ice. Shake well and strain into a chilled martini glass. Garnish with a maraschino cherry.

Buckeye Martini

6 parts Gin
1 part Dry Vermouth
1 Black Olive

Combine liquid ingredients in a cocktail shaker with cracked ice. Shake well and strain into a chilled martini glass. Garnish with a black olive.

Cabaret Martini

6 parts Gin
3 parts Dubonnet Rouge
3 to 5 dashes Angostura
    Bitters
3 to 5 dashes Pernod
1 Lime Twist

Combine liquid ingredients in a cocktail shaker with cracked ice. Shake well and strain into a chilled martini glass. Garnish with a lime twist.

Carousel Martini

2 oz. Gin
1 oz. White Creme de Cacao
2 dashes Grenadine
1 oz. Light Cream

Combine ingredients in a cocktail shaker with cracked ice. Shake and strain into a chilled martini glass.

Century Martini

2 oz. Gin
1 oz. Grapefruit Juice
1/2 oz. Chambord
1/2 oz. Triple Sec

Combine ingredients in a mixing glass with cracked ice. Shake and strain into a chilled martini glass.

Chateau Martini

3 oz. Gin
1/2 oz. Chambord
1 Orange Twist

Combine liquid ingredients in a cocktail shaker with cracked ice. Shake and strain into a chilled martini glass. Garnish with an orange twist.

Cherry Pink Lady Martini

2 oz. Gin
1 tsp. Cherry Brandy
1 tsp. Grenadine
1/2 oz. Heavy Cream

Combine ingredients in a cocktail shaker with cracked ice. Shake and strain into a chilled martini glass.

Christmas Martini

6 parts Gin
1 part Dry Vermouth
1 tsp. Peppermint Schnapps
1 Miniature Candy Cane

Combine liquid ingredients in a cocktail shaker with cracked ice. Shake well and strain into a chilled martini glass. Garnish with a candy cane.

Church Lady Martini

4 parts Gin
2 parts Dry Vermouth
2 parts Fresh Orange Juice
Lemon, Lime, and Orange
  Wedges

Combine liquid ingredients in a cocktail shaker with cracked ice. Shake well and strain into a chilled martini glass. Garnish with fruit wedges.

Churchill's Martini

6 parts Gin
1 Cocktail Olive

Pour gin in a cocktail shaker with cracked ice. Shake and strain into a chilled martini glass. Garnish with an olive. Note: This martini does not use any vermouth.

Classic Gin Martini

3 1/2 oz. Tanqueray Dry Gin
1 tsp. Dry Vermouth
1 Lemon Twist or Olive

Combine liquid ingredients in a mixing glass with cracked ice. Stir to chill and strain into a chilled martini glass. Garnish with a lemon twist or olive.

Colony Club Martini

6 parts Gin
1 tsp. Pernod
3 to 5 dashes Orange Bitters
1 Orange Twist

Combine liquid ingredients in a cocktail shaker with cracked ice. Shake well and strain into a chilled martini glass. Garnish with an orange twist.

Commedia Dell'Arte Martini

2 oz. Gin
1 oz. Galliano
1/2 oz. Black Sambuca

Combine ingredients in a mixing glass with cracked ice. Stir to chill and strain into a chilled martini glass.

Crantini Martini

6 parts Gin
1 part Unsweetened
  Cranberry Juice
1 Lime or Lemon Twist

Pour gin into a chilled martini glass. Slowly add cranberry juice. Garnish with a lime or lemon twist.

Crimson Martini

6 parts Gin
1 part Ruby Port
2 tsp Fresh Lime Juice
1 tsp Grenadine
1 Lime Twist

Combine liquid ingredients in a cocktail shaker with cracked ice. Shake well and strain into a chilled martini glass. Garnish with a lime twist.

Deep Sea Martini

6 parts Gin
2 parts Dry Vermouth
1/2 tsp. Pernod
1 dash Orange Bitters

Combine ingredients in a
mixing glass with cracked
ice. Stir well and strain into
a chilled martini glass.

Delancey Martini

2 oz. Gin
1 oz. Absolut Peppar
1 oz. Olive Juice
3 Olives

Combine liquid ingredients
in a mixing glass with
cracked ice. Stir to chill and
strain into a chilled martini
glass. Garnish with three
olives.

Delmonico Martini

1 1/2 oz. Gin
1/2 oz. Brandy
1/2 oz. Sweet Vermouth
2 dashes Angostura Bitters

Combine ingredients in a
mixing glass with cracked
ice. Stir to chill and strain
into a chilled martini glass.

Desperate Martini

6 parts Gin
1 part Dry Vermouth
1 part Blackberry Brandy
Fresh Blackberries
  (optional)

Combine liquid ingredients
in a cocktail shaker with
cracked ice. Shake well and
strain into a chilled martini
glass. Garnish with fresh
blackberries.

Dirty Gin Martini

3 oz. Gin
1/2 oz. Olive Juice
1 dash Dry Vermouth
3 Olives

Combine liquid ingredients in a mixing glass with cracked ice. Stir to chill and strain into a chilled martini glass. Garnish with three olives.

Dirty Martini

6 parts Gin
2 parts Dry Vermouth
1 part Olive Brine
Cocktail Olives

Combine liquid ingredients in a cocktail shaker with cracked ice. Shake well and strain into a chilled martini glass. Garnish with one or two olives.

Dry Martini

1 2/3 oz. Gin
1/3 oz. Dry Vermouth
1 Olive

Combine liquid ingredients in a mixing glass with cracked ice. Stir to chill and strain into a chilled martini glass. Garnish with an olive.

Elvira Martini

2 oz. Gin
1/2 oz. Dry Vermouth
1 tsp. Blue Curacao
2 dashes Orange Bitters

Combine ingredients in a mixing glass with cracked ice. Stir to chill and strain into a chilled martini glass.

Emerald Martini

1 1/2 oz. Gin
1/2 oz. Dry Vermouth
1/8 oz. Green Chartreuse
1 Twist Lemon Peel

Combine liquid ingredients in a cocktail shaker with cracked ice. Shake well and strain into a chilled martini glass. Twist a lemon zest over the drink and garnish by floating the zest on top.

Fare Thee Well Martini

6 parts Gin
1 part Dry Vermouth
1 dash Sweet Vermouth
1 dash Cointreau

Combine ingredients in a mixing glass with cracked ice. Stir well and strain into a chilled martini glass.

Farmer's Martini

6 parts Gin
1 part Dry Vermouth
1 part Sweet Vermouth
3 to 5 dashes Angostura
   Bitters

Combine ingredients in a cocktail shaker with cracked ice. Shake well and strain into a chilled martini glass.

Faust Martini

4 oz. Gin
3 dashes Tabasco Sauce
Chili Pepper

Combine liquid ingredients in a mixing glass with cracked ice. Stir to chill and strain into a chilled martini glass. Garnish with a couple dashes of chili pepper.

FDR's Martini

2 parts Gin
1 part Vermouth
1 tsp. Olive Brine
1 Lemon Twist
1 Cocktail Olive

Rub a lemon twist around the rim of a chilled martini glass and discard the peel. Combine gin, vermouth, and olive brine in a cocktail shaker with cracked ice. Shake well and strain into the martini glass. Garnish with an olive.

Fifty-Fifty Martini

4 parts Gin
4 parts Dry Vermouth
1 Cocktail Olive

Combine liquid ingredients in a cocktail shaker with cracked ice. Shake well and strain into a chilled martini glass. Garnish with an olive.

Fine and Dandy Martini

4 parts Gin
2 parts Triple Sec
2 parts Fresh Lemon Juice
1 dash Orange Bitters

Combine liquid ingredients in a cocktail shaker with cracked ice. Shake well and strain into a chilled martini glass.

Fino Martini

6 parts Gin
1 tsp. Fino Sherry
1 Lemon Twist

Combine liquid ingredients in a mixing glass with cracked ice. Stir well and strain into a chilled martini glass. Garnish with a lemon twist.

Fretful Martini

6 parts Gin
1 part Blue Curacao
1 dash Angostura Bitters
1 Cocktail Olive

Combine liquid ingredients in a cocktail shaker with cracked ice. Shake well and strain into a chilled martini glass. Garnish with an olive.

Frozen Martini

5 parts Gin
1 part Dry Vermouth
2 Almond-Stuffed Cocktail
  Olives

Place gin, vermouth, olives, martini glass, and cocktail shaker in a freezer for at least 3 hours. When all components are thoroughly chilled, combine gin and vermouth in the chilled cocktail shaker and shake well. Place the two frozen olives in a chilled martini glass and pour the gin and vermouth mixture over it.

Gibson Martini

8 parts Gin
3 to 5 dashes Dry Vermouth
2 Cocktail Onions

Combine liquid ingredients in a mixing glass with cracked ice. Stir well and strain into a chilled martini glass. Garnish with cocktail onions.

Gin Gibson Martini

3 oz. Gin
1/2 oz. Dry Vermouth
3 Cocktail Onions

Combine liquid ingredients in a mixing glass with cracked ice. Stir to chill and strain into a chilled martini glass. Garnish with three cocktail onions.

Gin Gimlet Martini

3 oz. Gin
1/2 oz. Roses Lime Juice
1 Lemon Wedge

Combine liquid ingredients in a mixing glass with cracked ice. Stir to chill and strain into a chilled martini glass. Garnish with a lemon wedge.

Golden Drop Martini

3 1/2 oz. Tanqueray 10 Gin
1 tsp. Dry Vermouth
3 drops Scotch
1 Lemon Twist or Olive

Combine liquid ingredients in a mixing glass with cracked ice. Stir to chill and strain into a chilled martini glass. Garnish with a lemon twist or olive.

Golf Martini

8 parts Gin
3 to 5 dashes Angostura
   Bitters
2 parts Dry Vermouth
1 Cocktail Olive

Combine liquid ingredients in a cocktail shaker with cracked ice. Shake well and strain into a chilled martini glass. Garnish with an olive.

Green Martini

6 parts Gin
1 part Chartreuse
1 Almond-Stuffed Olive

Combine liquid ingredients in a cocktail shaker with cracked ice. Shake well and strain into a chilled martini glass. Garnish with an olive.

Green River Martini

2 1/2 oz. Gin
1/2 oz. Green Chartreuse
1/2 oz. Yellow Chartreuse

Combine ingredients in a mixing glass with cracked ice. Stir to chill and strain into a chilled martini glass.

Green Widow Martini

2 1/2 oz. Gin
1 oz. Midori
1/2 oz. Fresh Sour Mix
1 splash Champagne

Combine ingredients, except champagne, in a cocktail shaker with cracked ice. Shake and strain into a chilled martini glass. Splash with champagne.

Gypsy Martini

8 parts Gin
2 parts Sweet Vermouth
1 Maraschino Cherry

Combine liquid ingredients in a cocktail shaker with cracked ice. Shake well and strain into a chilled martini glass. Garnish with a maraschino cherry.

Hasty Martini

6 parts Gin
1 part Dry Vermouth
3 to 5 dashes Pernod
1 tsp. Grenadine

Combine ingredients in a cocktail shaker with cracked ice. Shake well and strain into a chilled martini glass.

Haunted Bride Martini

1 1/2 oz. Gin
1 oz. Dry Vermouth
1/2 oz. Benedictine
1 tsp. Pernod
2 dashes Bitters

Combine ingredients in a mixing glass with cracked ice. Stir to chill and strain into a chilled martini glass.

Hoffman House Martini

8 parts Gin
1 part Dry Vermouth
3 to 5 dashes Orange Bitters
1 Cocktail Olive

Combine liquid ingredients in a cocktail shaker with cracked ice. Shake well and strain into a chilled martini glass. Garnish with an olive.

Hollywood Martini

6 parts Gin
1 part Goldwasser
1 part Dry Vermouth
1 Blue Cheese-Stuffed Olive

Combine liquid ingredients in a cocktail shaker with cracked ice. Shake well and strain into a chilled martini glass. Garnish with an olive.

Homer's Choice Martini

2 1/2 oz. Gin
1 oz. Ouzo

Combine ingredients in a mixing glass with cracked ice. Stir to chill and strain into a chilled martini glass.

Homestead Martini

6 pars Gin
2 parts Sweet Vermouth
1 Orange Twist

Combine liquid ingredients in a cocktail shaker with cracked ice. Shake well and strain into a chilled martini glass. Garnish with an orange twist.

Hotel Plaza Cocktail

2 parts Gin
2 parts Dry Vermouth
2 parts Sweet Vermouth
1 Maraschino Cherry

Combine liquid ingredients in a cocktail shaker with cracked ice. Shake well and strain into a chilled martini glass. Garnish with a maraschino cherry.

Ideal Martini

6 parts Gin
2 parts Dry Vermouth
1/2 tsp. Maraschino
   Liqueur
1 tsp. Fresh Lemon Juice
1 Lemon Twist

Combine liquid ingredients in a cocktail shaker with cracked ice. Shake well and strain into a chilled martini glass. Garnish with a lemon twist.

Imperial Martini

6 parts Gin
2 parts Dry Vermouth
1/2 tsp. Maraschino
   Liqueur
3 to 5 dashes Angostura
   bitters

Combine ingredients in a mixing glass with cracked ice. Stir well and strain into a chilled martini glass.

Jamaican Martini

6 parts Gin
1 part Red Wine
1 tbsp. Dark Rum
3 to 5 dashes Orange Bitters
Cherry Peppers

Combine liquid ingredients in a cocktail shaker with cracked ice. Shake well and strain into a chilled martini glass. Garnish with cherry peppers.

James Bond Martini

6 parts Gin
2 parts Vodka
1 part Lillet Blanc
1 Lemon Twist

Combine liquid ingredients in a cocktail shaker with cracked ice. Shake well and strain into a chilled martini glass. Garnish with a lemon twist.

Journalist Martini

6 parts Gin
1 tsp. Dry Vermouth
1 tsp. Sweet Vermouth
1 tsp. Triple Sec
1 tsp. Fresh Lime Juice
1 dash Angostura Bitters

Combine ingredients in a cocktail shaker with cracked ice. Shake well and strain into a chilled martini glass.

Knickerbocker Martini

6 parts Gin
2 parts Dry Vermouth
1/2 tsp. Sweet Vermouth
1 Lemon Twist

Combine liquid ingredients in a cocktail shaker with cracked ice. Shake well and strain into a chilled martini glass. Garnish with a lemon twist.

Kyoto Cocktail

6 parts Gin
2 parts Melon Liqueur
1 part Dry Vermouth
1/4 tsp. Fresh Lemon Juice
1 Melon Ball

Combine liquid ingredients in a cocktail shaker with cracked ice. Shake well and strain into a chilled martini glass. Garnish with a melon ball.

London Martini

6 parts Gin
1/2 tsp. Maraschino
  Liqueur
3 to 5 dashes Orange Bitters
1/2 tsp. Bar Sugar
1 Lemon Twist

Combine liquid ingredients in a cocktail shaker with cracked ice. Shake well and strain into a chilled martini glass. Garnish with a lemon twist.

Maritime Martini

6 parts Gin
2 parts Dry Vermouth
1 Anchovy-Stuffed Olive

Combine liquid ingredients in a cocktail shaker with cracked ice. Shake well and strain into a chilled martini glass. Garnish with an olive.

Martian Martini

2 oz. Gin
1 oz. Midori Melon Liqueur

Combine ingredients in a cocktail shaker with cracked ice. Shake gently and strain into a chilled martini glass.

Martinez Martini

1 1/2 oz. Gin
1 1/2 oz. Dry Vermouth
2 dashes Maraschino
  Liqueur
1 dash Bitters
1 Lemon Twist

Combine liquid ingredients in a mixing glass with cracked ice. Stir gently and serve in a chilled martini glass. Garnish with a lemon twist.

Martini

6 parts Gin
1 part Dry Vermouth
1 Cocktail Olive

Combine liquid ingredients in a cocktail shaker with cracked ice. Shake well and strain into a chilled martini glass. Garnish with an olive.

Martini Milano

4 parts Gin
1 part Dry Vermouth
1 part Dry White Wine
1 tsp. Campari
1 Lime Twist

Combine liquid ingredients in a cocktail shaker with cracked ice. Shake well and strain into a chilled martini glass. Garnish with a lime twist.

Martunia Martini

6 parts Gin
1 part Dry Vermouth
1 part Sweet Vermouth
Edible Flowers

Combine liquid ingredients in a cocktail shaker with cracked ice. Shake well and strain into a chilled martini glass. Garnish with edible flower pedals.

Naked Martini

6 parts Gin
1 Cocktail Olive

Chill the gin in a freezer for at least 2 hours. Pour gin into a chilled martini glass and garnish with an olive.

Napoleon Martini

3 oz. Gin
1/2 oz. Dubonnet Rouge
1/2 oz. Grand Marnier

Combine ingredients in a mixing glass with cracked ice. Stir to chill and strain into a chilled martini glass.

Nature Girl Martini

2 oz. Gin
1 oz. Triple Sec
1 tsp. Blue Curacao
1 dash Orange Bitters

Combine ingredients in a mixing glass with cracked ice. Stir to chill and strain into a chilled martini glass.

Negroni Martini

4 parts Gin
2 parts Campari
1 part Sweet Vermouth
1 Orange Twist

Combine liquid ingredients in a cocktail shaker with cracked ice. Shake well and strain into a chilled martini glass. Garnish with an orange twist.

Newbury Martini

6 parts Gin
2 parts Sweet Vermouth
1 part Triple Sec
1 Lemon Twist

Combine liquid ingredients in a cocktail shaker with cracked ice. Shake well and strain into a chilled martini glass. Garnish with a lemon twist.

Nightmare Martini

6 parts Gin
2 parts Madeira Wine
2 parts Cherry Brandy
1 Orange Twist

Combine liquid ingredients in a cocktail shaker with cracked ice. Shake well and strain into a chilled martini glass. Garnish with an orange twist.

Octopus's Garden Martini

6 parts Gin
2 parts Dry Vermouth
1 Smoked Baby Octopus
1 Black Olive

Combine liquid ingredients in a cocktail shaker with cracked ice. Shake well and strain into a chilled martini glass. Garnish with an olive and octopus.

Opal Martini

6 parts Gin
1 part Triple Sec
2 parts Fresh Orange Juice
1/4 tsp. Bar Sugar

Combine ingredients in a cocktail shaker with cracked ice. Shake well and strain into a chilled martini glass.

Opera Martini

6 parts Gin
2 parts Dubonnet Blanc
1 part Maraschino Liqueur
1 Lemon Twist

Combine liquid ingredients in a cocktail shaker with cracked ice. Shake well and strain into a chilled martini glass. Garnish with a lemon twist.

Orange Blossom Martini

2 oz. Gordon's Gin
2 oz. Orange Juice
1 tsp. Superfine Sugar
1 Orange Twist

Combine ingredients, except the orange twist, in a cocktail shaker with cracked ice. Shake and strain into a chilled martini glass. Garnish with an orange twist.

Paisley Martini

6 parts Gin
1/2 tsp. Dry Vermouth
1/2 tsp. Scotch
1 Cocktail Olive

Combine liquid ingredients in a cocktail shaker with cracked ice. Shake well and strain into a chilled martini glass. Garnish with an olive.

Pall Mall Martini

4 parts Gin
1 part Dry Vermouth
1 part Sweet Vermouth
1 tsp. White Creme de Menthe
1 dash Orange Bitters

Combine ingredients in a cocktail shaker with cracked ice. Shake well and strain into a chilled martini glass.

Palm Beach Martini

6 parts Gin
1 tsp. Sweet Vermouth
4 parts Grapefruit Juice

Combine ingredients in a cocktail shaker with cracked ice. Shake well and strain into a chilled martini glass.

Paris Opera Martini

2 oz. Tanqueray 10 Gin
1 oz. Dubonnet Rouge
3 dashes Orange Bitters
1 Orange Twist

Combine liquid ingredients in a mixing glass with cracked ice. Stir to chill and strain into a chilled martini glass. Garnish with an orange twist.

Parisian Martini

6 parts Gin
2 parts Dry Vermouth
1 part Creme de Cassis

Combine ingredients in a cocktail shaker with cracked ice. Shake well and strain into a chilled martini glass.

Park Avenue Martini

6 parts Gin
1 part Sweet Vermouth
1 part Pineapple Juice

Combine ingredients in a cocktail shaker with cracked ice. Shake well and strain into a chilled martini glass.

Perfect Martini

6 parts Gin
1 part Dry Vermouth
1 part Sweet Vermouth
1 Cocktail Olive

Combine liquid ingredients in a cocktail shaker with cracked ice. Shake well and strain into a chilled martini glass. Garnish with an olive.

Picadilly Martini

6 parts Gin
2 parts Dry Vermouth
1/2 tsp. Pernod
1 dash Grenadine

Combine ingredients in a mixing glass with cracked ice. Stir gently and strain into a chilled martini glass.

Pink Gin Martini

8 parts Gin
1 tsp. Angostura Bitters

Pour bitters into a chilled martini glass and swirl around until the inside of the glass is completely coated. Pour gin into the glass. Do not chill the ingredients.

Pink Lady Martini

2 oz. Gin
1 oz. White Creme de Cacao
1 tsp. Grenadine
1/2 oz. Heavy Cream

Combine ingredients in a mixing glass with cracked ice. Shake and strain into a chilled martini glass.

Pink Panther Martini

2 oz. Gin
1 oz. Campari
1/2 oz. Grapefruit Juice
1/2 oz. Champagne

Combine ingredients, except champagne, in a cocktail shaker with cracked ice. Shake and strain into a chilled martini glass. Top with champagne.

Pink Rose Martini

1 tsp. Powdered sugar
2 oz. Gin
1 oz. Apricot Brandy
1 oz. Lime Juice
1 Lime Wedge

Moisten the rim of a chilled martini glass with lime wedge and dip into a bowl of sugar. Combine gin, brandy and juice in a mixing glass with cracked ice. Stir to chill and strain into the martini glass.

Pink Squirrelly Martini

2 oz. Gin
1 oz. Creme de Noyaux
1 tsp. Grenadine
1 oz. Light Cream

Combine ingredients in a cocktail shaker with cracked ice. Shake and strain into a chilled martini glass.

Plaza Martini

2 parts Gin
2 parts Dry Vermouth
2 parts Sweet Vermouth

Combine ingredients in a cocktail shaker with cracked ice. Shake well and strain into a chilled martini glass.

Prince Edward Martini

6 parts Gin
1 part Drambuie
1 Lemon Twist

Combine liquid ingredients in a cocktail shaker with cracked ice. Shake well and strain into a chilled martini glass. Garnish with a lemon twist.

Queen Elizabeth Martini

6 parts Gin
1 part Dry Vermouth
2 tsp. Benedictine

Combine ingredients in a cocktail shaker with cracked ice. Shake well and strain into a chilled martini glass.

Queen's Ruby Martini

2 oz. Barton London Extra
  Dry Gin
1/2 oz. Cherry Brandy
1 tsp. Sweet Vermouth

Combine ingredients in a mixing glass with cracked ice. Stir to chill and strain into a chilled martini glass.

Racquet Club Martini

6 parts Gin
2 parts Dry Vermouth
3 to 5 dashes Orange Bitters

Combine ingredients in a cocktail shaker with cracked ice. Shake well and strain into a chilled martini glass.

Gin Martinis

Renaissance Martini

6 parts Gin
1 part Fino Sherry
Grated Nutmeg

Combine liquid ingredients in a cocktail shaker with cracked ice. Shake well and strain into a chilled martini glass. Garnish with nutmeg.

Rendezvous Martini

6 parts Gin
2 parts Cherry Brandy
1 part Campari
1 Fresh Cherry

Combine liquid ingredients in a cocktail shaker with cracked ice. Shake well and strain into a chilled martini glass. Garnish with a fresh cherry.

Resolution Martini

6 parts Gin
2 parts Apricot Brandy
1 part Fresh Lemon Juice

Combine ingredients in a cocktail shaker with cracked ice. Shake well and strain into a chilled martini glass.

Rolls Royce Martini

6 parts Gin
2 parts Dry Vermouth
2 parts Sweet Vermouth
1/4 tsp. Benedictine

Combine ingredients in a cocktail shaker with cracked ice. Shake well and strain into a chilled martini glass.

Saketini Martini

6 parts Gin
1 part Sake
1 Lemon Twist wrapped
   with Pickled Ginger

Combine liquid ingredients
in a cocktail shaker with
cracked ice. Shake well and
strain into a chilled martini
glass. Garnish with a lemon
twist.

Secret Martini

6 parts Gin
2 parts Lillet Blanc
2 dashes Angostura Bitters
1 Cocktail Olive

Combine liquid ingredients
in a cocktail shaker with
cracked ice. Shake well and
strain into a chilled martini
glass. Garnish with an olive.

Seventh Heaven Martini

6 parts Gin
1 part Maraschino Liqueur
1 part Grapefruit Juice
1 Fresh Mint Sprig

Combine liquid ingredients
in a cocktail shaker with
cracked ice. Shake well and
strain into a chilled martini
glass. Garnish with a mint
sprig.

Sexy Maiden Martini

2 1/2 oz. Gin
1 oz. Cointreau
1 tsp. Blue Curacao
1 oz. Fresh Sour Mix
1 oz. Grapefruit Juice

Combine ingredients in a
mixing glass with cracked
ice. Shake and strain into a
chilled martini glass.

Shrimptini Martini

6 parts Gin
2 parts Dry Vermouth
Dash Tabasco Sauce
1 Large Cooked Shrimp

Combine liquid ingredients in a cocktail shaker with cracked ice. Shake well and strain into a chilled martini glass. Garnish with the cooked shrimp.

Silver Steak Martini

6 parts Gin
3 parts Jagermeister
1 Lemon Twist

Combine liquid ingredients in a cocktail shaker with cracked ice. Shake well and strain into a chilled martini glass. Garnish with a lemon twist.

Sloe Gin Martini

6 parts Sloe Gin
2 parts Dry Vermouth
3 to 5 dashes Angostura
  Bitters
1 Lemon Twist

Combine liquid ingredients in a cocktail shaker with cracked ice. Shake well and strain into a chilled martini glass. Garnish with a lemon twist.

Smoky Martini

6 parts Gin
1 part Dry Vermouth
1 tsp. Scotch
1 Lemon Twist

Combine liquid ingredients in a cocktail shaker with cracked ice. Shake well and strain into a chilled martini glass. Garnish with a lemon twist.

Soho Martini

2 1/2 oz. Gin
1/2 oz. Chambord
1 oz. Sour Mix
1 Lemon Twist

Combine liquid ingredients in a cocktail shaker with cracked ice. Shake and strain into a chilled martini glass. Garnish with a lemon twist.

South Side Cocktail Martini

3 Mint Leaves
1 tsp. Superfine Sugar
2 oz. Gin
1 1/2 oz. Lemon Juice
1 Mint Sprig

Muddle mint leaves and sugar in the bottom of a mixing glass. Add gin, juice and cracked ice. Stir to chill and strain into a chilled martini glass. Garnish with a mint sprig.

Southern Martini

6 parts Gin
1 part Triple Sec
3 to 5 dashes Orange Bitters
1 Lemon Twist

Combine liquid ingredients in a cocktail shaker with cracked ice. Shake well and strain into a chilled martini glass. Garnish with a lemon twist.

Strawberry Martini

2 oz. Gin
1 tsp. Dry Vermouth
1 tsp. Rose's Grenadine
   Syrup
Sugar
Strawberries

Rub the rim of a chilled martini glass with a cut strawberry. Dip rim into a bowl of sugar until evenly coated. Combine liquid ingredients in a mixing glass with crushed ice. Stir well and strain into a chilled martini glass. Drop a strawberry into the martini.

Sweet Martini

6 parts Gin
2 parts Sweet Vermouth
1 dash Orange Bitters
1 Orange Twist

Combine liquid ingredients in a cocktail shaker with cracked ice. Shake well and strain into a chilled martini glass. Garnish with an orange twist.

Sweetie Martini

6 parts Gin
1 part Dry Vermouth
1 part Sweet Vermouth
1 Lemon Twist

Combine liquid ingredients in a cocktail shaker with cracked ice. Shake well and strain into a chilled martini glass. Garnish with a lemon twist.

The Academic Martini

2 oz. Gin
1/2 oz. Galliano
1/2 oz. Orange Juice

Combine ingredients in a mixing glass with cracked ice. Stir to chill and strain into a chilled martini glass.

The Cloisters Martini

1 1/2 oz. Gin
1/2 oz. Sweet Vermouth
1 oz. Campari
1 tsp. Benedictine
1 tsp. Pernod
2 dashes Bitters
1 Orange Twist

Combine liquid ingredients in a mixing glass with cracked ice. Stir to chill and strain into a chilled martini glass. Garnish with an orange twist.

The Crater Martini

2 oz. Gin
1 oz. Dark Creme de Cacao
1/2 oz. Chambord
1/2 oz. Heavy Cream

Combine ingredients in a cocktail shaker with cracked ice. Shake and strain into a chilled martini glass.

Third Degree Martini

6 parts Gin
2 parts Dry Vermouth
1 part Pernod
Star Anise

Combine liquid ingredients in a cocktail shaker with cracked ice. Shake well and strain into a chilled martini glass. Garnish with star anise.

Three Stripes Martini

4 parts Gin
2 parts Dry Vermouth
2 parts Fresh Orange Juice

Combine ingredients in a cocktail shaker with cracked ice. Shake well and strain into a chilled martini glass.

Triton Martini

2 oz. Gin
1 oz. Triple Sec
1 oz. White Creme de Cacao
1/2 tsp. Blue Curacao

Combine ingredients in a mixing glass with cracked ice. Stir to chill and strain into a chilled martini glass.

Turf Martini

4 parts Gin
2 parts Dry Vermouth
1 part Pernod
1 part Fresh Lemon Juice
3 to 5 dashes Angostura
  Bitters
1 Almond-Stuffed Olive

Combine liquid ingredients in a cocktail shaker with cracked ice. Shake well and strain into a chilled martini glass. Garnish with an olive.

Wembly Martini

6 parts Gin
1 part Dry Vermouth
1 tsp. Apricot Brandy
1 tsp. Calvados
1 Lemon Twist

Combine liquid ingredients in a cocktail shaker with cracked ice. Shake well and strain into a chilled martini glass. Garnish with a lemon twist.

VODKA

MARTINIS

43

Abra Cadabra Martini

2 oz. Vodka
1/2 oz. Peach Schnapps
1/2 oz. Apricot Brandy
1 oz. Pineapple Juice

Combine ingredients in a mixing glass with cracked ice. Stir to chill and strain into a chilled martini glass.

Absolut Martini

5 parts Absolut Vodka
1 part Triple Sec
2 parts Fresh Lemon Juice
1 dash Orange Bitters

Combine ingredients in a cocktail shaker with cracked ice. Shake well and strain into a chilled martini glass.

Alize Martini

2 1/2 oz. Alize Liqueur
1 oz. Vodka

Combine ingredients in a mixing glass with cracked ice. Stir well and strain into a chilled martini glass.

Alternatini Martini

6 parts Vodka
1/2 tsp. Sweet Vermouth
1/2 tsp. Dry Vermouth
1 tsp. White Creme de Cacao
Sweetened Cocoa Powder
Hershey's Kiss

Rim a chilled martini glass with sweetened cocoa powder. Combine liquid ingredients in a cocktail shaker with cracked ice. Shake well and strain into the martini glass. Garnish with a Hershey's Kiss.

Ambrosia Martini

2 oz. Vodka
1 oz. Apricot Schnapps
1 oz. Peach Juice
1/2 oz. Light Cream

Combine ingredients in a mixing glass with cracked ice. Shake and strain into a chilled martini glass.

Apple Martini

2 oz. Vodka
1 1/2 oz. Bols Sour Apple
   Liqueur
1/2 oz. Lemon Juice
1 Apple Slice

Combine liquid ingredients in a mixing glass with cracked ice. Stir to chill and strain into a chilled martini glass. Garnish with an apple slice.

Apple Pie Martini

6 parts Vanilla-Flavored
   Vodka
1 part Calvados
1 part Dry Vermouth
1 Apple Slice

Combine liquid ingredients in a cocktail shaker with cracked ice. Shake well and strain into a chilled martini glass. Garnish with a thin apple slice.

Armada Martini

6 parts Vodka
2 parts Amontillado Sherry
1 Orange Twist

Combine liquid ingredients in a mixing glass with cracked ice. Stir to chill and strain into a chilled martini glass. Garnish with an orange twist.

Aztec Gold Martini

1 oz. Absolut
1 oz. Jose Cuervo Gold
   Tequila
1 oz. Mount Gay Rum
1 oz. Pineapple Juice

Combine ingredients in mixing glass with cracked ice. Stir to chill and strain into a chilled martini glass.

Babyface Martini

6 parts Strawberry-
   Flavored Vodka
1 part Dry Vermouth
1/2 tsp. Maraschino
   Liqueur
1 Fresh Strawberry

Combine liquid ingredients in a cocktail shaker with cracked ice. Shake well and strain into a chilled martini glass. Garnish with a fresh strawberry.

Banana Split Martini

1 oz. Vodka
1 oz. Creme de Banane
1 oz. Godiva White
   Chocolate Liqueur
1/2 oz. Strawberry Syrup
1/2 oz. Heavy Cream
1 Strawberry

Combine liquid ingredients in mixing glass with cracked ice. Shake and strain into a chilled martini glass. Garnish with a strawberry.

Bananarama Martini

2 oz. Vodka
1 oz. Creme de Banane
1/2 oz. White Creme de
   Cacao
1/2 oz. Light Cream
2 drops Yellow Food
   Coloring

Combine ingredients in cocktail shaker with cracked ice. Shake and strain into a chilled martini glass.

Barbed Wire Martini

6 parts Vodka
1 tsp. Sweet Vermouth
1/2 tsp. Pernod
1/2 tsp. Chambord
1 Lemon Twist

Combine liquid ingredients in a cocktail shaker with cracked ice. Shake well and strain into a chilled martini glass. Garnish with a lemon twist.

Basic Vodka Martini

3 oz. Vodka
1 tsp. Dry Vermouth
1 Lemon Twist or 3 Olives

Combine liquid ingredients in a mixing glass with cracked ice. Stir to chill and strain into a chilled martini glass. Garnish with a lemon twist or three olives.

Bellini Martini

3 oz. Vodka
1 1/2 oz. Peach Nectar
1 1/2 oz. Peach Schnapps
1 Twist Lemon Peel

Combine liquid ingredients in a cocktail shaker with cracked ice. Shake gently and strain into a chilled martini glass. Garnish with a twist of lemon peel.

Berlin Martini

2 oz. Smirnoff Vodka
3 dashes Apple Schnapps
1 splash Black Sambuca
1 Blackberry

Combine liquid ingredients in a cocktail shaker with cracked ice. Shake gently and strain into a chilled martini glass. Garnish with a blackberry.

48

Berrytini Martini

6 parts Currant Vodka
1 part Raspberry Eau-de-
  Vie
Fresh Raspberries

Combine liquid ingredients
in a cocktail shaker with
cracked ice. Shake well and
strain into a chilled martini
glass. Garnish with fresh
raspberries.

Birth of Venus Martini

2 oz. Vodka
1 oz. Cointreau
1 tsp. Blue Curacao
1 oz. Peach Juice
1 oz. Champagne

Combine ingredients,
except champagne, in a
mixing glass with cracked
ice. Stir to chill and strain
into a chilled martini glass.
Top with champagne and
stir gently.

Black & White Martini

6 parts Vanilla Vodka
2 parts Creme de Cacao
Black & White Licorice
  Candies

Combine liquid ingredients
in a cocktail shaker with
cracked ice. Shake well and
strain into a chilled martini
glass. Garnish with black
and white licorice candies.

Blavod Martini

2 1/2 oz. Blavod Vodka
1/2 oz. Sweet Vermouth
1 Maraschino Cherry

Combine liquid ingredients
in a cocktail shaker with
cracked ice. Shake well and
strain into a chilled martini
glass. Garnish with a
maraschino cherry.

Blue Angel Martini

2 oz. Vodka
1 oz. Blue Curacao
1 oz. White Creme de Cacao

Combine ingredients in a mixing glass with cracked ice. Stir to chill and strain into a chilled martini glass.

Blue Ape Martini

2 oz. Vodka
1 oz. Creme de Banane
1 oz. White Creme de Cacao
1/2 tsp. Blue Curacao

Combine ingredients in a mixing glass with cracked ice. Stir to chill and strain into a chilled martini glass.

Blue Inca Martini

2 oz. Vodka
1 oz. Silver Tequila
1 oz. Light Rum
1 oz. Blue Curacao

Combine ingredients in a mixing glass with cracked ice. Stir to chill and strain into a chilled martini glass.

Blue Orange Martini

2 oz. Vodka
1 oz. Blue Curacao
1 oz. Cointreau

Combine ingredients in a mixing glass with cracked ice. Stir to chill and strain into a chilled martini glass.

Blue-on-Blue Martini

6 parts Vodka
1 part Blue Curacao
1 dash Angostura Bitters
1 Cocktail Olive

Combine liquid ingredients in a cocktail shaker with cracked ice. Shake well and strain into a chilled martini glass. Garnish with an olive.

Bluebird Martini

3 oz. Vodka
1 oz. Blue Curacao

Combine ingredients in a mixing glass with cracked ice. Stir to chill and strain into a chilled martini glass.

Boardwalk Martini

6 parts Vodka
2 parts Dry Vermouth
1/2 tsp. Maraschino
   Liqueur
1 tsp. Fresh Lemon Juice
1 Lemon Twist

Combine liquid ingredients in a cocktail shaker with cracked ice. Shake well and strain into a chilled martini glass. Garnish with a lemon twist.

Breakfast Martini

2 oz. Vodka
2 tbsp. Marmalade

Combine ingredients in a cocktail shaker with crushed ice. Shake well and strain into a chilled martini glass.

Cajun Martini

6 parts Pepper Vodka
1 dash Dry Vermouth
Olive stuffed with pickled
  Jalapeno Pepper

Combine liquid ingredients
in a cocktail shaker with
cracked ice. Shake well and
strain into a chilled martini
glass. Garnish with an olive.

California Martini

6 parts Vodka
1 part Red Wine
1 tbsp. Dark Rum
3 to 5 dashes Orange Bitters
1 Orange Twist

Combine liquid ingredients
in a cocktail shaker with
cracked ice. Shake well and
strain into a chilled martini
glass. Garnish with an
orange twist.

Campari Martini

6 parts Vodka
1 part Campari
1 Lime Twist

Combine liquid ingredients
in a cocktail shaker with
cracked ice. Shake well and
strain into a chilled martini
glass. Garnish with a lime
twist.

Candy Cane Martini

1/2 oz. Vodka
1/2 oz. Absolut Peppar
1 oz. Sambuca
1 oz. White Creme de
  Menthe
1 oz. White Creme de Cacao

Combine ingredients in a
mixing glass with cracked
ice. Stir to chill and strain
into a chilled martini glass.

Caribou Martini

4 parts Coffee-Flavored
  Vodka, chilled
Champagne or Dry
  Sparkling Wine
1 Lemon Twist
1 Coffee Bean

Pour chilled vodka into a chilled martini glass. Top with champagne and stir gently. Garnish with a lemon twist and drop in a coffee bean.

Cherry Pie Martini

2 oz. Vodka
1 oz. Brandy
1 oz. Cherry Brandy

Combine ingredients in mixing glass with cracked ice. Stir to chill and strain into a chilled martini glass.

Chocolate Banana Martini

2 parts Vodka
1 part Creme de Cacao
1 part 99 Bananas (99 proof
  banana liqueur)
1 Hershey's Kiss

Combine liquid ingredients in a mixing glass with cracked ice. Stir well and strain into a chilled martini glass. Garnish with a Hershey's Kiss or Godiva Chocolate.

Chocolate Martini

6 parts Vodka
1 part Chocolate Liqueur
1 Chocolate Curl

Combine liquid ingredients in a mixing glass with cracked ice. Stir to chill and strain into a chilled martini glass. Garnish with a chocolate curl.

Chocolate Vodka Martini

2 oz. Vodka
1 oz. Godiva Liqueur
1 oz. White Creme de Cacao
1 Chocolate Stick (optional)

Combine liquid ingredients in a mixing glass with cracked ice. Stir to chill and strain into a chilled martini glass. Garnish with a chocolate stick (optional).

Christmas Tini Martini

6 parts Vodka
1 tsp. Peppermint Schnapps
1 part Dry Vermouth
1 Miniature Candy Cane

Combine liquid ingredients in a cocktail shaker with cracked ice. Shake well and strain into a chilled martini glass. Garnish with a candy cane.

Citrus Martini

8 parts Lemon-Flavored
  Vodka
1 tsp Grand Marnier or
  Orange Liqueur
1 tsp Fresh Lime Juice
1 Lemon Twist

Combine liquid ingredients in a cocktail shaker with cracked ice. Shake well and strain into a chilled martini glass. Garnish with a lemon twist.

Coffee Lover's Martini

6 parts Coffee-Flavored
  Vodka
1 part Dry Vermouth
1 part Frangelico
Coffee Beans

Combine liquid ingredients in a cocktail shaker with cracked ice. Shake well and strain into a chilled martini glass. Garnish with a few coffee beans.

Cold Comfort Martini

4 parts Lemon Vodka
4 parts Honey Vodka
1 Lemon Twist

Combine ingredients in a cocktail shaker with cracked ice. Shake well and strain into a chilled martini glass. Garnish with a lemon twist.

Cosmopolitan Martini

2 oz. Vodka
1 oz. Cointreau
1/2 oz. Cranberry Juice
1/2 oz. Fresh Sour Mix
1 Lemon Twist

Combine liquid ingredients in a cocktail shaker with cracked ice. Shake and strain into a chilled martini glass. Garnish with a lemon twist.

Creamsicle Martini

2 oz. Vodka
1 oz. Triple Sec
1 oz. Orange Juice
1 oz. Heavy Cream
1 Orange Slice

Combine ingredients in a cocktail shaker with cracked ice. Shake and strain into a chilled martini glass. Garnish with an orange slice.

Creamy Dream Martini

2 oz. Vodka
1 oz. Grand Marnier
1/2 oz. Creme de Cassis
1/2 oz. Light Cream

Combine ingredients in a cocktail shaker with cracked ice. Shake and strain into a chilled martini glass. Garnish with fruit of your choice.

Daydream Martini

6 parts Citrus Vodka
1 part Triple Sec
2 parts Fresh Orange Juice
1/4 tsp. Bar Sugar

Combine ingredients in a mixing glass with cracked ice. Stir well and strain into a chilled martini glass.

Delicious Martini

6 parts Coffee-Flavored
  Vodka
1 part Grand Marnier
1 Orange Twist

Combine liquid ingredients in a cocktail shaker with cracked ice. Shake well and strain into a chilled martini glass. Garnish with an orange twist.

Delilah Martini

2 oz. Stoli Ohranj
1 oz. Cointreau
1 oz. White Creme de Cacao
1/2 tsp. Grenadine

Combine ingredients in a mixing glass with cracked ice. Stir to chill and strain into a chilled martini glass.

Dirty Blonde Martini

2 oz. Vodka
1 oz. Johnnie Walker Gold
  Label
1 oz. Drambuie

Combine ingredients in a mixing glass with cracked ice. Stir to chill and strain into a chilled martini glass.

Dirty Vodka Martini

6 parts Vodka
2 parts Dry Vermouth
1 part Olive Brine
Cocktail Olives

Combine liquid ingredients in a cocktail shaker with cracked ice. Shake well and strain into a chilled martini glass. Garnish with one or two olives.

Double Fudge Martini

6 parts Vodka
1 part Chocolate Liqueur
1 part Coffee Liqueur
1 Chocolate Cocktail Straw

Combine liquid ingredients in a cocktail shaker with cracked ice. Shake well and strain into a chilled martini glass. Garnish with a chocolate straw.

Dry Sherry Martini

2 oz. Vodka
1/2 oz. Dry Vermouth
1/2 oz. Dry Sherry
1 Lemon Twist

Combine liquid ingredients in a mixing glass with cracked ice. Stir to chill and strain into a chilled martini glass. Garnish with a lemon twist.

East Wing Martini

6 parts Vodka
1 part Campari
2 parts Cherry Brandy
1 Lemon Twist

Combine liquid ingredients in a cocktail shaker with cracked ice. Shake well and strain into a chilled martini glass. Garnish with a lemon twist.

Eat My Martini

6 parts Honey Vodka
1 part Amontillado Sherry
1 Almond-Stuffed Olive

Combine liquid ingredients in a cocktail shaker with cracked ice. Shake well and strain into a chilled martini glass. Garnish with an olive.

Emerald Vodka Martini

1 1/2 oz. Vodka
1/2 oz. Dry Vermouth
1/8 oz. Green Chartreuse
1 Twist Lemon Peel

Combine liquid ingredients in a cocktail shaker with cracked ice. Shake well and strain into a chilled martini glass. Twist a lemon zest over the drink and garnish by floating the zest on top.

Extra Dry Martini

4 parts Vodka
3 to 5 drops Dry Vermouth
1/8 tsp. Lemon Juice
1 Lemon Twist

Combine liquid ingredients in a cocktail shaker with cracked ice. Shake well and strain into a chilled martini glass. Garnish with a lemon twist.

Fifty-Fifty Vodka Martini

4 parts Vodka
4 parts Dry Vermouth
1 Cocktail Olive

Combine liquid ingredients in a cocktail shaker with cracked ice. Shake well and strain into a chilled martini glass. Garnish with an olive.

Fino Martini

6 parts Vodka
1 tsp. Fino Sherry
1 Lemon Twist

Combine liquid ingredients in a mixing glass with cracked ice. Stir well and strain into a chilled martini glass. Garnish with a lemon twist.

French Martini

2 oz. Vodka
1 oz. Chambord
1 1/2 oz. Pineapple Juice

Combine ingredients in mixing glass with cracked ice. Stir to chill and strain into a chilled martini glass.

Flirtini Martini

1 1/2 oz. Vodka
1/2 oz. Triple Sec
1/2 oz. Cranberry Juice
1/2 oz. Lemon Juice
1/2 tsp. Sugar
1 oz. Champagne
1 Orange Twist

Combine vodka, triple sec, juices and sugar in cocktail shaker with cracked ice. Shake and strain into a chilled martini glass. Top with champagne and stir gently. Garnish with an orange twist.

Fuzzy Martini

4 parts Vanilla-Flavored
  Vodka
1 part Coffee-Flavored
  Vodka
1 tsp. Peach Schnapps
1 Fresh Peach Slice

Combine liquid ingredients in a mixing glass with cracked ice. Stir gently and strain into a chilled martini glass. Garnish with a fresh peach slice.

Gibson Martini

8 parts Vodka
3 to 5 dashes Dry Vermouth
2 Cocktail Onions

Combine liquid ingredients in a mixing glass with cracked ice. Stir well and strain into a chilled martini glass. Garnish with cocktail onions.

Gilroy Martini

6 parts Buffalo Grass Vodka
2 parts Dry Vermouth
2 drops Garlic Juice
1 Garlic-Stuffed Olive

Combine liquid ingredients in a cocktail shaker with cracked ice. Shake well and strain into a chilled martini glass. Garnish with an olive.

Gimlet Martini

8 parts Gin or Vodka
2 parts Rose's Lime Juice

Combine ingredients in a cocktail shaker with cracked ice. Shake well and strain into a chilled martini glass.

Godchild Martini

1 oz. Vodka
1 oz. Amaretto
1 oz. Heavy Cream

Combine ingredients in a cocktail shaker with cracked ice. Shake and strain into a chilled martini glass.

Great Caesar's Martini

6 parts Vodka
1 part Dry Vermouth
1 Anchovy-Stuffed Olive

Combine liquid ingredients in a cocktail shaker with cracked ice. Shake well and strain into a chilled martini glass. Garnish with an olive.

Greensleeves Martini

2 oz. Vodka
1 oz. Irish Mist
1 oz. Green Creme de
   Menthe

Combine ingredients in a mixing glass with cracked ice. Stir to chill and strain into a chilled martini glass.

Hazelnut Martini

1 oz. Ketel One Vodka
1/2 oz. Frangelico Hazelnut
   Liqueur

Combine ingredients in a mixing glass with cracked ice. Stir to chill and strain into a chilled martini glass.

Hep Cat Martini

6 parts Berry Vodka
1 part Dry Vermouth
1 dash Sweet Vermouth
1 dash Cointreau

Combine ingredients in a mixing glass with cracked ice. Stir well and strain into a chilled martini glass.

Honeydew Martini

6 parts Vodka
1 part Midori
1 part Triple Sec
1 Lemon Twist

Combine liquid ingredients in a cocktail shaker with cracked ice. Shake well and strain into a chilled martini glass. Garnish with a lemon twist.

Hoosier Cocktail

4 parts Buffalo Grass Vodka
2 parts Light Rum
1 part Dry Vermouth

Combine ingredients in a mixing glass with cracked ice. Stir well and strain into a chilled martini glass.

Hot & Dirty Martini

6 parts Pepper Vodka
1 part Dry Vermouth
1 tsp. Olive Brine
Olive stuffed with pickled
   Jalapeno Pepper

Combine liquid ingredients in a cocktail shaker with cracked ice. Shake well and strain into a chilled martini glass. Garnish with an olive.

Irish Martini

6 parts Buffalo Grass Vodka
1 part Dry Vermouth
Irish Whiskey
1 Lemon Twist

Rinse a chilled martini glass with irish whiskey. Combine vodka and vermouth in a cocktail shaker with cracked ice. Shake well and strain into the chilled martini glass. Garnish with a lemon twist.

Jack London Martini

6 parts Currant Vodka
2 parts Dubonnet Blanc
1 part Maraschino Liqueur
1 Lemon Twist

Combine liquid ingredients in a cocktail shaker with cracked ice. Shake well and strain into a chilled martini glass. Garnish with a lemon twist.

James Bond Martini

6 parts Gin
2 parts Vodka
1 part Lillet Blanc
1 Lemon Twist

Combine liquid ingredients in a cocktail shaker with cracked ice. Shake well and strain into a chilled martini glass. Garnish with a lemon twist.

Jubilee Martini

2 oz. Grey Goose Vodka
1/2 oz. Cointreau
1 oz. Fresh Sour Mix
2 Mint Leaves, crushed
1 Mint Sprig

Combine vodka, Cointreau, sour mix and mint leaves in a mixing glass with cracked ice. Shake well and strain into a chilled martini glass. Garnish with a mint sprig.

Kojak Martini

2 oz. Vodka
1 oz. X-RATED Fusion
  Liqueur
1 drop Vermouth
few drops Lime Juice
1 Tootsie Pop lollypop
  (Cherry)

Combine vodka, vermouth and X-RATED Fusion Liqueur in a cocktail shaker with cracked ice. Shake well and strain into a chilled martini glass. Add a few drops of lime juice. Drop in a cherry Tootsie Pop upside down like Kojak use to eat. This is an original ShotDrinks.com cocktail.

Leap Year Martini

6 parts Citrus-Flavored
  Vodka
1 part Sweet Vermouth
1 part Grand Marnier
1/2 tsp. Fresh Lemon Juice

Combine ingredients in a
cocktail shaker with cracked
ice. Shake well and strain
into a chilled martini glass.

Lemon Cosmopolitan Martini

2 oz. Absolut Lemon
1 oz. Cointreau
1 oz. Cranberry Juice
1 Lemon Twist

Combine liquid ingredients
in a cocktail shaker with
cracked ice. Shake and
strain into a chilled martini
glass. Garnish with a lemon
twist.

Lemon Drop Martini

6 parts Lemon-Flavored
  Vodka
1 part Dry Vermouth
Granulated Sugar
1 Lemon Twist

Rim a chilled martini glass
with granulated sugar.
Combine liquid ingredients
in a cocktail shaker with
cracked ice. Shake well and
strain into the chilled
martini glass. Garnish with
a lemon twist.

Lemon Splash Martini

1 1/2 oz. Vodka
1/2 oz. Triple Sec
1/2 oz. Amaretto Almond
  Liqueur
Juice 1 Lemon Wedge
1 twist Lemon Peel

Combine liquid ingredients
in a cocktail shaker with
cracked ice. Shake gently
and strain into a chilled
martini glass. Garnish with
a lemon twist.

Low Tide Martini

6 parts Vodka
1 part Dry Vermouth
1 tsp. Clam Juice
1 Olive stuffed with Smoked
   Clam
1 Lime Twist

Combine liquid ingredients
in a cocktail shaker with
cracked ice. Shake well and
strain into a chilled martini
glass. Garnish with an olive
and lime twist.

Macaroon Martini

6 parts Vodka
1 part Chocolate Liqueur
1 part Amaretto
1 Orange Twist

Combine liquid ingredients
in a cocktail shaker with
cracked ice. Shake well and
strain into a chilled martini
glass. Garnish with an
orange twist.

Mama's Martini

6 parts Vanilla Vodka
1 part Apricot Brandy
3 to 5 dashes Angostura
   Bitters
3 to 5 dashes Lemon Juice

Combine ingredients in a
cocktail shaker with cracked
ice. Shake well and strain
into a chilled martini glass.

Merry Berry Martini

2 oz. Stoli Razberi
1 oz. Chambord
1/2 oz. Sloe Gin
1/2 oz. Lemon Juice

Combine ingredients in a
mixing glass with cracked
ice. Stir to chill and strain
into a chilled martini glass.

Metropolitan Martini

6 parts Currant Vodka
1 part Lillet Blanc
1/2 tsp. Fresh Lime Juice
1 Lemon Twist

Combine liquid ingredients in a cocktail shaker with cracked ice. Shake well and strain into a chilled martini glass. Garnish with a lemon twist.

Mocha Blanca Martini

6 parts Coffee-Flavored
  Vodka
2 parts White Chocolate
  Liqueur
1 White Chocolate Curl

Combine liquid ingredients in a cocktail shaker with cracked ice. Shake well and strain into a chilled martini glass. Garnish with a chocolate curl.

Monkey Martini

1 1/2 oz. Vodka
1 oz. Creme de Banane
1 oz. Dark Creme de Cacao
1/2 oz. Light Cream

Combine ingredients in a cocktail shaker with cracked ice. Shake and strain into a chilled martini glass.

Mount Etna Martini

2 oz. Absolut Peppar
1 oz. Tomato Juice
1 oz. Sambuca
2 dashes Tabasco Sauce

Combine ingredients in a mixing glass with cracked ice. Stir to chill and strain into a chilled martini glass.

Mudslide Martini

1 oz. Vodka
1 oz. Bailey's Irish Cream
1 oz. Dark Creme de Cacao

Combine vodka and liqueur in a mixing glass with cracked ice. Stir to chill and strain into a chilled martini glass. Slowly drizzle creme de cacao down the inside of the glass.

Neon Light Martini

1 1/2 oz. Vodka
1/2 oz. Yellow Chartreuse
2 tsp. Galliano
2 tsp. Blue Curacao
1/2 tsp. Lemon Juice
1 Maraschino Cherry

Combine liquid ingredients in a mixing glass with cracked ice. Stir to chill and strain into a chilled martini glass. Garnish with a maraschino cherry.

New Orleans Martini

6 parts Vanilla Vodka
1 part Dry Vermouth
1 part Pernod
1 dash Angostura Bitters
1 Fresh Mint Sprig

Combine liquid ingredients in a cocktail shaker with cracked ice. Shake well and strain into a chilled martini glass. Garnish with a mint sprig.

Nuts & Berries Martini

2 oz. Absolut Kurant
1 oz. Frangelico
1/2 oz. Chambord
1/2 oz. Dark Creme de
  Cacao
1/2 oz. Light Cream

Combine ingredients in a cocktail shaker with cracked ice. Shake and strain into a chilled martini glass.

Nutty Martini

6 parts Vodka
1 part Frangelico
1 Lemon Twist

Combine liquid ingredients in a cocktail shaker with cracked ice. Shake well and strain into a chilled martini glass. Garnish with a lemon twist.

Old Country Martini

6 parts Vodka
2 parts Madeira Wine
2 parts Cherry Brandy
1 Orange Twist

Combine liquid ingredients in a cocktail shaker with cracked ice. Shake well and strain into a chilled martini glass. Garnish with an orange twist.

Orange Cosmopolitan Martini

2 oz. Absolut Orange
1 oz. Cointreau
1 oz. Cranberry Juice
1 oz. Fresh Sour Mix
1 Orange Twist

Combine liquid ingredients in a mixing glass with cracked ice. Shake and strain into a chilled martini glass. Garnish with an orange twist.

Orange Martini

6 parts Vodka
1 part Triple Sec
1 dash Orange Bitters
1 Orange Twist

Combine liquid ingredients in a cocktail shaker with cracked ice. Shake well and strain into a chilled martini glass. Garnish with an orange twist.

Osaka Dry Martini

6 parts Vodka
1 part Sake
1 Pickled Plum

Combine liquid ingredients in a cocktail shaker with cracked ice. Shake well and strain into a chilled martini glass. Garnish with a pickled plum.

Oyster Martini

6 parts Vodka
1 part Dry Vermouth
1 Smoked Oyster

Combine liquid ingredients in a cocktail shaker with cracked ice. Shake well and strain into a chilled martini glass. Garnish with a smoked oyster on a toothpick.

Peach Blossom Martini

6 parts Peach Vodka
1 part Dubonnet Rouge
1 part Maraschino Liqueur
1 Fresh Peach Slice

Combine liquid ingredients in a cocktail shaker with cracked ice. Shake well and strain into a chilled martini glass. Garnish with a peach slice.

Peachy Martini

6 parts Strawberry-
   Flavored Vodka
2 parts Peach Brandy
1 Lemon Twist

Combine liquid ingredients in a cocktail shaker with cracked ice. Shake well and strain into a chilled martini glass. Garnish with a lemon twist.

Peppermint Martini

6 parts Pepper Vodka
2 parts White Creme de
  Menthe
1 Fresh Mint Sprig

Combine liquid ingredients
in a cocktail shaker with
cracked ice. Shake well and
strain into a chilled martini
glass. Garnish with a mint
sprig.

Percolator Martini

1 oz. Vodka
1 oz. Cognac
1 oz. Grand Marnier
1 oz. White Creme de Cacao

Combine ingredients in a
mixing glass with cracked
ice. Stir to chill and strain
into a chilled martini glass.

Pink Martini

1 1/4 oz. Grey Goose Vodka
1/4 oz. Lime Juice
1/4 oz. Triple Sec
1/4 oz. Cranberry Juice
1 Lime Slice

Combine ingredients in a
cocktail shaker with cracked
ice. Shake and strain into a
chilled martini glass.
Garnish with a lime slice.

Pink Squirrel Martini

1 oz. Creme de Cacao
1 oz. Creme de Noyaux
1/2 oz. Skyy Vodka
1 oz. Heavy Cream

Combine ingredients in a
cocktail shaker with cracked
ice. Shake and strain into a
chilled martini glass.

Pomegranate Martini

1/2 cups Pomegranate Juice
2 oz. Absolute Citron Vodka
1 oz. Cointreau Liquor
Splash Sparkling Water
Squeeze Lemon
1 Pomegranate Fruit Slice

Combine liquid ingredients in a cocktail shaker with cracked ice. Shake and strain into a chilled martini glass. Garnish with a pomegranate fruit slice inside the drink.

Pretty Martini

4 parts Vodka
1 part Grand Marnier
1 part Amaretto
1 part Dry Vermouth
1 Orange Twist

Combine liquid ingredients in a cocktail shaker with cracked ice. Shake well and strain into a chilled martini glass. Garnish with an orange twist.

Purple Passion Martini

2 oz. Vodka
3 oz. Red Grape Fruit Juice
1/2 tsp. Superfine Sugar

Combine ingredients in a mixing glass with cracked ice. Stir to chill and strain into a chilled martini glass.

Quarterdeck Martini

6 parts Berry Vodka
1 part Maraschino Liqueur
1 part Grapefruit Juice
1 Fresh Mint Sprig

Combine liquid ingredients in a cocktail shaker with cracked ice. Shake well and strain into a chilled martini glass. Garnish with a mint sprig.

Rasmopolitan Martini

2 oz. Raspberry-Flavored
  Vodka
1 oz. Cointreau
1 oz. Cranberry Juice
1 oz. Fresh sour mix
1 Lemon Twist

Combine liquid ingredients in a cocktail shaker with cracked ice. Shake and strain into a chilled martini glass. Garnish with a lemon twist.

Red Dog Martini

6 parts Vodka
1 part Ruby Port
2 tsp. Fresh Lime Juice
1 tsp. Grenadine
1 Lime Twist

Combine liquid ingredients in a cocktail shaker with cracked ice. Shake well and strain into a chilled martini glass. Garnish with a lime twist.

Road Runner Martini

6 parts Pepper Vodka
1 part Dry Vermouth
1 part Gold Tequila
1 Jalapeno Stuffed Olive

Combine liquid ingredients in a cocktail shaker with cracked ice. Shake well and strain into a chilled martini glass. Garnish with an olive.

Russian Martini

4 parts Vodka
4 parts Gin
1 part White Chocolate
  Liqueur

Combine liquid ingredients in a cocktail shaker with cracked ice. Shake well and strain into a chilled martini glass.

Russian Rose Martini

6 parts Strawberry-
  Flavored Vodka
1 part Dry Vermouth
1 part Grenadine
1 dash Orange Bitters

Combine ingredients in a mixing glass with cracked ice. Stir well and strain into a chilled martini glass.

Salt and Pepper Martini

1/8 oz. Vermouth
2 oz. Absolut Peppar

Combine ingredients in a mixing glass with cracked ice. Stir gently and strain into a chilled martini glass with a salted rim.

Sexy Devil Martini

4 parts Vodka
2 parts Cranberry Vodka
1 part Dry Vermouth
1 Lemon Peel
1 Fresh Strawberry

Combine liquid ingredients in a cocktail shaker with cracked ice. Shake well and strain into a chilled martini glass. Garnish with a lemon peel and fresh strawberry.

She Walks in Beauty Martini

3 oz. Ciroc Grape Vodka
1/2 oz. Chambord
1/2 oz. Apricot Brandy

Combine liquid ingredients in a mixing glass with cracked ice. Stir to chill and strain into a chilled martini glass. Garnish with a fruit of choice.

Shrimptini Martini

6 parts Vodka
2 parts Dry Vermouth
Dash Tabasco Sauce
1 Large Cooked Shrimp

Combine liquid ingredients
in a cocktail shaker with
cracked ice. Shake well and
strain into a chilled martini
glass. Garnish with the
cooked shrimp.

Silver Lining Martini

2 oz. Chopin Polish Vodka,
  chilled
2 Large Spanish Olives with
  Pimentos, marinated in
  Aquavit or Dry White
  Sherry

Pour a small amount of
aquavit or sherry into a well
chilled martini glass. Swirl
once and discard. Add
chilled vodka and garnish
with olives on a toothpick.

Snow Storm Martini

2 oz. Vodka
1 oz. Godiva White
  Chocolate Liqueur
1 oz. White Creme de Cacao

Combine ingredients in a
mixing glass with cracked
ice. Stir to chill and strain
into a chilled martini glass.

Sour Apple Martini

2 oz. Citrus Vodka
1/2 oz. DeKuyper Sour
  Apple Pucker Schnapps
1/2 oz. Cointreau orange
  liqueur
3/4 oz. Fresh Lemon Juice
1 Apple Slice

Combine liquid ingredients
in a cocktail shaker with
cracked ice. Shake gently
and strain into a chilled
martini glass. Garnish with
an apple slice.

Southern Angel Martini

2 oz. Vodka
1 oz. Southern Comfort
1 oz. Peach Juice
2 Mint Leaves, crushed
1/2 tsp. Superfine Sugar
1 Mint Sprig

Combine vodka, Southern Comfort, peach juice, mint leaves and sugar in a mixing glass with cracked ice. Shake and strain into a chilled martini glass. Garnish with a mint sprig.

Southern Skies Martini

1 oz. Vodka
1 oz. Light Rum
1 oz. Blue Curacao
1 oz. Pineapple Juice

Combine ingredients in a mixing glass with cracked ice. Stir to chill and strain into a chilled martini glass.

Soviet Martini

6 parts Ashberry-Flavored
  or Currant Vodka
1 part Dry Vermouth
1 part Fino Sherry
1 Lemon Twist

Combine liquid ingredients in a cocktail shaker with cracked ice. Shake well and strain into a chilled martini glass. Garnish with a lemon twist.

Spiced Treat Martini

6 parts Cinnamon Vodka
1 part Chocolate Liqueur
1 part Coffee Liqueur
1 Chocolate Cocktail Straw

Combine liquid ingredients in a cocktail shaker with cracked ice. Shake well and strain into a chilled martini glass. Garnish with a chocolate cocktail straw.

Springtime Martini

6 parts Buffalo Grass Vodka
2 parts Lillet Blanc
1 Miniature Pickled
   Asparagus Spear

Combine liquid ingredients
in a cocktail shaker with
cracked ice. Shake well and
strain into a chilled martini
glass. Garnish with an
asparagus spear.

St. Petersburg Martini

6 parts Vodka
3 to 5 dashes Orange Bitters
1 Orange Peel

Combine liquid ingredients
in a cocktail shaker with
cracked ice. Shake well and
strain into a chilled martini
glass. Garnish with an
orange peel.

Staten Island Cocktail

6 parts Coffee Vodka
1 part Dry Vermouth
2 parts Fresh Lime Juice
1 Maraschino Cherry

Combine liquid ingredients
in a cocktail shaker with
cracked ice. Shake well and
strain into a chilled martini
glass. Garnish with a
maraschino cherry.

Strawberry Blonde Martini

6 parts Strawberry Vodka
2 parts Lillet Blanc
1 Fresh Strawberry

Combine liquid ingredients
in a cocktail shaker with
cracked ice. Shake well and
strain into a chilled martini
glass. Garnish with a
strawberry.

Summer Breeze Martini

6 parts Citrus Vodka
2 parts Melon Liqueur
1 part Dry Vermouth
1/4 tsp. Fresh Lemon Juice
1 Melon Ball

Combine liquid ingredients in a cocktail shaker with cracked ice. Shake well and strain into a chilled martini glass. Garnish with a melon ball.

Summer Cooler Martini

3 Mint Sprigs
1 tsp. Superfine Sugar
1 oz. Lemon Juice
2 1/2 oz. Vodka
1 Mint Sprig

Muddle three mint sprigs, sugar, lemon juice, and vodka in the bottom of a mixing glass. Add cracked ice and shake. Strain into a chilled martini glass and garnish with a mint sprig.

Summer Snap Martini

2 oz. Vodka
1/2 oz. White Creme de Menthe
1 oz. Apricot Brandy
1/2 oz. Lemon Juice
1 Mint Sprig

Combine liquid ingredients in a mixing glass with cracked ice. Stir to chill and strain into a chilled martini glass. Garnish with a mint sprig.

Sweet and Spicy Martini

6 parts Cinnamon Vodka
1 part Sweet Vermouth
1 part Orange Liqueur
1 Cinnamon Stick

Combine liquid ingredients in a cocktail shaker with cracked ice. Shake well and strain into a chilled martini glass. Garnish with a cinnamon stick.

Swiss Alps Martini

1 oz. Vodka
1 oz. Godiva White
   Chocolate Liqueur
1 oz. White Creme de Cacao
1 oz. Light Cream
Chocolate Shavings

Combine liquid ingredients in a mixing glass with cracked ice. Shake and strain into a chilled martini glass. Garnish with chocolate shavings.

Tanhauser Martini

2 oz. Vodka
1 oz. Dark Creme de Cacao
1/2 oz. Light Cream
1/2 oz. Jagermeister

Combine ingredients in a cocktail shaker with cracked ice. Shake and strain into a chilled martini glass.

The Blue Period Martini

2 oz. Ketel One Vodka
1 oz. Southern Comfort
1/2 oz. Pernod
1/2 oz. Blue Curacao
1/2 oz. Chambord

Combine ingredients in a mixing glass with cracked ice. Stir to chill and strain into a chilled martini glass.

The Potion Martini

2 oz. Vodka
1 oz. Chambord
1/2 oz. Lemon Juice
1/2 tsp. Superfine Sugar

Combine ingredients in a cocktail shaker with cracked ice. Shake and strain into a chilled martini glass.

The Sophisticated Metropolitan Martini

1 1/2 oz. Absolut Kurant
1 oz. Cointreau
1/2 oz. Chambord
1 oz. Fresh Sour Mix
1 oz. Cranberry Juice
1 Lemon Twist

Combine liquid ingredients in a mixing glass with cracked ice. Stir to chill and strain into a chilled martini glass. Garnish with a lemon twist.

The Warsaw Martini

2 oz. Lukusowa Potato Vodka
1 oz. Hiram Walker Blackberry Brandy
1 oz. Dry Vermouth
1 tsp. Lemon Juice

Combine ingredients in a cocktail shaker with cracked ice. Shake and strain into a chilled martini glass.

Thundercloud Martini

2 oz. Vodka
1/2 oz. Chambord
1/2 oz. Blue Curacao
1/2 oz. Heavy Cream

Combine ingredients in a cocktail shaker with cracked ice. Shake and strain into a chilled martini glass.

Tootsie Roll Martini

6 parts Vodka
1 part Chocolate Liqueur
1 part Grand Marnier
1 Orange Twist

Combine liquid ingredients in a cocktail shaker with cracked ice. Shake well and strain into a chilled martini glass. Garnish with an orange twist.

Topaz Martini

2 oz. Vodka
1 oz. Orange Juice
1 oz. Apricot Brandy

Combine ingredients in a mixing glass with cracked ice. Stir to chill and strain into a chilled martini glass.

Truffle Martini

6 parts Strawberry Vodka
1 part Grand Marnier
1 part Chocolate Liqueur
1 Orange Twist

Combine liquid ingredients in a cocktail shaker with cracked ice. Shake well and strain into a chilled martini glass. Garnish with an orange twist.

Truffly Martini

2 oz. Vodka
1 oz. Dark Creme de Cacao
1/2 tsp. Chambord
1 oz. Heavy Cream

Combine ingredients in a mixing glass with cracked ice. Shake and strain into a chilled martini glass.

Tutti Frutti Martini

1 oz. Grey Goose Orange
  Vodka
1 oz. Stoli Razberi
1 oz. Chambord
1 oz. Orange Juice
1 oz. Cranberry Juice

Combine ingredients in a mixing glass with cracked ice. Stir to chill and strain into a chilled martini glass.

Tuxedo Martini

4 parts Vodka
3 parts Dry Vermouth
1/2 tsp. Maraschino
  Liqueur
3 to 5 dashes Orange Bitters
1 Lemon Twist

Combine liquid ingredients in a cocktail shaker with cracked ice. Shake well and strain into a chilled martini glass. Garnish with a lemon twist.

Vanilla Twist Martini

6 parts Vanilla Vodka
1 part Cointreau
1 part Dry Vermouth
1 Vanilla Bean

Combine liquid ingredients in a cocktail shaker with cracked ice. Shake well and strain into a chilled martini glass. Garnish with a vanilla bean.

Velvet Hammer Martini

2 oz. Vodka
1 oz. White Creme de Cacao
1 oz. Light Cream

Combine ingredients in a cocktail shaker with cracked ice. Shake and strain into a chilled martini glass.

Viva Europa Martini

1 1/2 oz. Vodka
1/2 oz. Amaretto
1/2 oz. Cointreau
1/2 oz. Galliano
1 oz. Orange Juice
1 oz. Pineapple Juice
2 dashes Bitters

Combine ingredients in a mixing glass with cracked ice. Stir to chill and strain into a chilled martini glass.

Vodka Damsel Martini

1 oz. Vodka
1 oz. Stoli Razberi
1 oz. Grapefruit Juice
1 oz. Peach Schnapps

Combine ingredients in a mixing glass with cracked ice. Stir to chill and strain into a chilled martini glass.

Vodka Gibson Martini

3 oz. Vodka
1 tsp. Dry Vermouth
3 Cocktail Onions

Combine liquid ingredients in a mixing glass with cracked ice. Stir to chill and strain into a chilled martini glass. Garnish with three cocktail onions.

Vodka Grasshopper Martini

1 oz. Vodka
1 oz. Green Creme de Menthe
1 oz. White Creme de Cacao

Combine ingredients in a mixing glass with cracked ice. Stir to chill and strain into a chilled martini glass.

Vodka Hopper Martini

2 oz. Vodka
1 oz. Green Creme de Menthe
1/2 oz. Light Cream
1 Mint Sprig

Combine liquid ingredients in a cocktail shaker with cracked ice. Shake and strain into a chilled martini glass. Garnish with a mint sprig.

Vodka Martini

6 parts Vodka
2 parts Dry Vermouth (or to
  taste)
1 Olive

Combine liquid ingredients
in a cocktail shaker with
cracked ice. Shake well and
strain into a chilled martini
glass. Garnish with an olive.

Vodka Negroni Martini

2 1/2 oz. Vodka
1 1/2 oz. Campari
1/2 oz. Sweet Vermouth

Combine ingredients in a
mixing glass with cracked
ice. Stir to chill and strain
into a chilled martini glass.

Vodka Orange Blossom Martini

2 oz. Stoli Ohranj
1 oz. Cointreau
1 oz. Orange Juice
2 dashes Orange Bitters

Combine ingredients in a
mixing glass with cracked
ice. Stir to chill and strain
into a chilled martini glass.

Vodka Refresher Martini

2 oz. Absolut Citron
1 oz. Fresh Sour Mix
4 oz. Tonic Water
1 Lime Wedge

Combine vodka and sour
mix in a mixing glass with
cracked ice. Shake and
strain into a chilled martini
glass. Add tonic water and
garnish with a lime wedge.

Vodka Stinger Martini

2 1/2 oz. Vodka
1 1/2 oz. White Creme de
  Menthe

Combine ingredients in a mixing glass with cracked ice. Stir to chill and strain into a chilled martini glass.

Waikiki Martini

6 parts Pineapple Vodka
1 part Dry Vermouth
1 part Lillet Blanc
1 Pineapple Wedge

Combine liquid ingredients in a cocktail shaker with cracked ice. Shake well and strain into a chilled martini glass. Garnish with a pineapple wedge.

Warsaw Martini

4 parts Potato Vodka
1 part Dry Vermouth
1 part Blackberry Brandy
1 tbsp. Fresh Lemon Juice

Combine ingredients in a cocktail shaker with cracked ice. Shake well and strain into a chilled martini glass.

Watermelon Candy Martini

1 oz. Vodka
1/2 oz. Melon Liqueur
1/2 oz. Cranberry Juice
Grenadine

Combine vodka, melon and cranberry juice in a cocktail shaker with cracked ice. Shake well. Swirl a splash of vermouth in a chilled martini glass and pour out. Strain shaker into the martini glass and add a splash of grenadine. This is an original ShotDrinks.com.

Watermelon Martini

1/2 oz. Fresh Lemon Juice
1 oz. Midori Melon Liqueur
1 oz. Citrus Vodka
1 1/2 oz. Fresh Watermelon
   Juice
1 Mint Sprig

Combine liquid ingredients in a cocktail shaker with crushed ice. Shake gently and strain into a chilled martini glass. Garnish with a sprig of mint.

Wedding Cake Martini

2 oz. Vanilla Vodka
1 oz. Pineapple Juice
1 oz. Cranberry Juice
1 tsp. Artificial Sweetner

Combine ingredients in a cocktail shaker with cracked ice. Shake well and strain into a chilled martini glass.

White Licorice Martini

2 oz. Vodka
1 oz. White Creme de Cacao
1/2 oz. Sambuca
1/2 oz. Light Cream

Combine ingredients in a cocktail shaker with cracked ice. Shake and strain into a chilled martini glass.

Wicked Monk Martini

1 1/2 oz. Vodka
1 oz. Frangelico
1/2 oz. Blue Curacao
1/2 oz. Southern Comfort

Combine ingredients in a mixing glass with cracked ice. Stir to chill and strain into a chilled martini glass.

Woo Woo Martini

6 parts Cranberry Vodka
1 part Peach Schnapps
1 Lemon Twist

Combine liquid ingredients in a cocktail shaker with cracked ice. Shake well and strain into a chilled martini glass. Garnish with a lemon twist.

X-Rated Flirtini

1 part X-Rated Fusion
1 part X-Rated Vodka
1 Lemon Slice

Combine ingredients in a cocktail shaker with crushed ice. Shake gently and strain into a chilled martini glass. Garnish with a lemon slice.

Xena Martini

5 parts Honey-Flavored
  Vodka
1 part Buffalo Grass Vodka
1 tsp. Lillet Blanc
1 Pickled Asparagus Spear

Combine liquid ingredients in a cocktail shaker with cracked ice. Shake well and strain into a chilled martini glass. Garnish with an asparagus spear.

Zippy Martini

6 parts Vodka
1 part Dry Vermouth
3 to 4 dashes Tabasco Sauce
1 Pickled Jalapeno Pepper
  Slice

Combine liquid ingredients in a cocktail shaker with cracked ice. Shake well and strain into a chilled martini glass. Garnish with a pepper slice.

RUM

MARTINIS

Applesauce Martini

2 oz. Gold Rum
1 oz. Applejack
1 tsp. Cinnamon
1 Apple Slice

Combine rum, applejack
and cinnamon in a mixing
glass with cracked ice. Stir
to chill and strain into a
chilled martini glass.
Garnish with an apple slice.

Aztec Gold Martini

1 oz. Absolut
1 oz. Jose Cuervo Gold
  Tequila
1 oz. Mount Gay Rum
1 oz. Pineapple Juice

Combine ingredients in
mixing glass with cracked
ice. Stir to chill and strain
into a chilled martini glass.

Bacardi O Tini

1 1/2 oz. Bacardi Orange
  Rum
3/4 oz. Pineapple Juice
Raspberry Liqueur

Combine ingredients,
except raspberry liqueur, in
a cocktail shaker with
cracked ice. Shake and
strain into a chilled martini
glass. Float raspberry
liqueur on top.

Banana Cream Pie Martini

2 oz. Light Rum
1/2 oz. Creme de Banane
1/2 oz. Godiva Liqueur
1/2 oz. White Creme de
  Cacao

Combine ingredients in a
mixing glass with cracked
ice. Stir to chill and strain
into a chilled martini glass.

Black Dog Martini

6 parts Light Rum
1 part Dry Vermouth
1 Pitted Black Olive

Combine liquid ingredients in a mixing glass with cracked ice. Stir well and strain into a chilled martini glass. Garnish with an olive.

Blind Kamikaze Martini

2 oz. Light Rum
1/2 oz. Peach Schnapps
1/2 oz. Midori
1/2 oz. Chambord
1 Lemon Twist

Combine liquid ingredients in a mixing glass with cracked ice. Stir to chill and strain into a chilled martini glass. Garnish with a lemon twist.

Blue Inca Martini

2 oz. Vodka
1 oz. Silver Tequila
1 oz. Light Rum
1 oz. Blue Curacao

Combine ingredients in a mixing glass with cracked ice. Stir to chill and strain into a chilled martini glass.

Candy Apple Martini

2 oz. Dark Rum
1/2 oz. Sour Apple Liqueur
1/2 oz. Cherry Heering
1/2 oz. Lemon Juice
1 Maraschino cherry

Combine ingredients in a mixing glass with cracked ice. Stir to chill and strain into a chilled martini glass. Garnish with a maraschino cherry.

Caribbean Sunset Martini

2 oz. Light Rum
1/2 oz. Triple Sec
1/2 oz. Lemon Juice
1 Lemon Twist

Combine liquid ingredients in a mixing glass with cracked ice. Stir to chill and strain into a chilled martini glass. Garnish with a lemon twist.

Caribbean Twilight Martini

2 oz. Dark Rum
1/2 oz. Orange Liqueur
1/2 oz. Lemon Juice
1 dash Peychaud's Bitters
1 Orange Twist

Combine liquid ingredients in a mixing glass with cracked ice. Stir to chill and strain into a chilled martini glass. Garnish with an orange twist.

Chocolate Mint Cocktail Martini

2 oz. Light Rum
1/2 oz. White Creme de Menthe
1/2 oz. Godiva Liqueur
1 Mint Sprig

Combine liquid ingredients in a mixing glass with cracked ice. Stir to chill and strain into a chilled martini glass. Garnish with a mint sprig.

Chocolate-Covered Orange Martini

2 oz. Gold Rum
1/2 oz. Cointreau
1/2 oz. Godiva Liqueur
1 Orange Twist

Combine liquid ingredients in a mixing glass with cracked ice. Stir to chill and strain into a chilled martini glass. Garnish with an orange twist.

Cuban Martini

6 parts Light Rum
1 part Dry Vermouth
Granulated Sugar
1 Lime Twist

Rim a chilled martini glass with sugar. Combine liquid ingredients in a cocktail shaker with cracked ice. Shake well and strain into the chilled martini glass. Garnish with a lime twist.

Daiquiri Martini

2 1/2 oz. Bacardi Light Rum
2 oz. Fresh Lime Juice
1 tsp. Superfine Sugar

Combine ingredients in a cocktail shaker with cracked ice. Shake and strain into a chilled martini glass.

Foreign Legion Martini

2 oz. Mount Gay Rum
1/2 oz. Dubonnet Rouge
1/2 oz. Orange Juice

Combine ingredients in a cocktail shaker with cracked ice. Shake and strain into a chilled martini glass. Optionally use orange juice with pulp instead of strained orange juice for a textured drink.

Foxy Squirrel Martini

2 oz. Light Rum
1/2 oz. Amaretto
1/2 oz. Creme de Noyaux
1/2 oz. Chambord

Combine ingredients in a mixing glass with cracked ice. Stir to chill and strain into a chilled martini glass.

Gumdrop Martini

4 parts Lemon-Flavored
  Rum
2 parts Vodka
1 part Southern Comfort
1/2 tsp. Dry Vermouth
1 part Fresh Lemon Juice
Bar Sugar
1 Lemon Slice
Gum Drops

Rim a chilled martini glass
with bar sugar. Combine
liquid ingredients in a
cocktail shaker with cracked
ice. Shake well and strain
into the chilled martini
glass. Garnish with a lemon
slice and gum drops.

Island Martini

6 parts Gold Rum
1 part Dry Vermouth
1 part Sweet Vermouth
1 Lemon Twist

Combine liquid ingredients
in a cocktail shaker with
cracked ice. Shake well and
strain into a chilled martini
glass. Garnish with a lemon
twist.

Hoosier Cocktail

4 parts Buffalo Grass Vodka
2 parts Light Rum
1 part Dry Vermouth

Combine ingredients in a
mixing glass with cracked
ice. Stir well and strain into
a chilled martini glass.

Lemon Meringue Martini

2 oz. Light Rum
1/2 oz. Limoncello
1/2 oz. Orange Liqueur
1/2 oz. Lemon Juice

Combine ingredients in a
cocktail shaker with cracked
ice. Shake and strain into a
chilled martini glass.

Lemon Twist Martini

6 parts Lemon-Flavored
  Rum
1 part Dry Vermouth
1 Lemon Twist

Combine liquid ingredients in a cocktail shaker with cracked ice. Shake well and strain into a chilled martini glass. Garnish with a lemon twist.

Ravishing Hazel Martini

2 1/2 oz. Gold Rum
1/2 oz. Frangelico
1/2 oz. Heavy Cream

Combine ingredients in a mixing glass with cracked ice. Shake and strain into a chilled martini glass.

Refreshing Breeze Martini

2 oz. Mount Gay Rum
1/2 oz. Cointreau
1/2 oz. Lemon Juice
3 Mint Sprigs, crushed
1 Mint Sprig

Combine rum, Countreau, lemon juice and three mint sprigs in a mixing glass with cracked ice. Stir well and strain into a chilled martini glass. Garnish with a mint sprig.

Rum Bluebird Martini

2 oz. Light Rum
1/2 oz. Blueberry Liqueur
1/2 oz. Fresh Sour Mix

Combine ingredients in a cocktail shaker with cracked ice. Shake and strain into a chilled martini glass.

Rum Jubilee Martini

3 Peppermint Sprigs
1/2 oz. Fresh Sour Mix
2 oz. Light Rum
1 Peppermint Sprig

Muddle three peppermint sprigs and sour mix in the bottom of a mixing glass. Add rum and cracked ice. Shake and strain into a chilled martini glass. Garnish with a peppermint sprig.

Rum Lover's Fruit Cup Martini

2 oz. Bacardi 151
1/2 oz. Orange Juice
1/2 oz. Cranberry Juice
1/2 oz. Lemon Juice

Combine ingredients in a mixing glass with cracked ice. Shake and strain into a chilled martini glass.

Rum Martini

6 parts Light Rum
1 part Dry Vermouth
1 dash Orange Bitters
1 Almond-Stuffed Olive

Combine liquid ingredients in a cocktail shaker with cracked ice. Shake well and strain into a chilled martini glass. Garnish with an olive.

Rum Martini

6 parts Light Rum
1 part Dry Vermouth
1 dash Orange Bitters
1 Almond-Stuffed Olive

Combine liquid ingredients in a cocktail shaker with cracked ice. Shake well and strain into a chilled martini glass. Garnish with an olive.

Rum Negroni Martini

2 oz. Light Rum
2 oz. Campari
2 oz. Sweet Vermouth
1 Orange Twist

Combine liquid ingredients in a mixing glass with cracked ice. Stir to chill and strain into a chilled martini glass. Garnish with an orange twist.

Rum Rico Martini

2 oz. Light Rum
1/2 oz. Red Grape Juice
1/2 oz. Raspberry Liqueur
1 White Grape

Combine liquid ingredients in a mixing glass with cracked ice. Stir to chill and strain into a chilled martini glass. Garnish with a white grape.

Rum Twister Martini

2 oz. Light Rum
1/2 oz. White Creme de
   Menthe
1/2 oz. Creme de Cacao
1 Lemon Twist

Combine liquid ingredients in a mixing glass with cracked ice. Stir to chill and strain into a chilled martini glass. Garnish with a lemon twist.

Rummy Meditation Martini

2 oz. Light Rum
1 oz. Benedictine
1 Lemon Twist

Combine liquid ingredients in a mixing glass with cracked ice. Stir to chill and strain into a chilled martini glass. Garnish with a lemon twist.

Rummy Southern Belle Martini

2 oz. Light Rum
1 1/2 oz. Peach Schnapps
1 1/2 oz. Southern Comfort
1 Peach Slice

Combine liquid ingredients in a mixing glass with cracked ice. Stir to chill and strain into a chilled martini glass. Garnish with a peach slice.

Senora Caesar Martini

2 oz. Light Rum
1/2 oz. Galliano
1/2 oz. Fresh Sour Mix
1 Lemon Twist

Combine liquid ingredients in a cocktail shaker with cracked ice. Shake and strain into a chilled martini glass. Garnish with a lemon twist.

Senora McGilliguddy Martini

2 oz. Light Rum
1/2 oz. Irish Mist
1/2 oz. Fresh Sour Mix
1 Lemon Twist

Combine liquid ingredients in a cocktail shaker with cracked ice. Shake and strain into a chilled martini glass. Garnish with a lemon twist.

Southern Skies Martini

1 oz. Vodka
1 oz. Light Rum
1 oz. Blue Curacao
1 oz. Pineapple Juice

Combine ingredients in a mixing glass with cracked ice. Stir to chill and strain into a chilled martini glass.

Squirrel's Nest Martini

2 oz. Dark Rum
1/2 oz. Amaretto
1/2 oz. Creme de Noyaux

Combine ingredients in a cocktail shaker with cracked ice. Shake and strain into a chilled martini glass.

The 1812 Martini

2 oz. Bacardi Silver
1/2 oz. Peach Schnapps
1/2 oz. Southern Comfort
1 Orange Twist

Combine liquid ingredients in a mixing glass with cracked ice. Stir to chill and sstrain into a chilled martini glass. Garnish with an orange twist.

Tijuana Express Martini

1 1/2 oz. Light Rum
1/2 oz. Dark Creme de
  Cacao
Whipped Cream

Combine liquid ingredients in a mixing glass with cracked ice. Shake and strain into a chilled martini glass. Top with whipped cream.

TEQUILA

MARTINIS

Aztec Gold Martini

1 oz. Absolut
1 oz. Jose Cuervo Gold
  Tequila
1 oz. Mount Gay Rum
1 oz. Pineapple Juice

Combine ingredients in mixing glass with cracked ice. Stir to chill and strain into a chilled martini glass.

Blue Inca Martini

2 oz. Vodka
1 oz. Silver Tequila
1 oz. Light Rum
1 oz. Blue Curacao

Combine ingredients in a mixing glass with cracked ice. Stir to chill and strain into a chilled martini glass.

Parrothead Martini

6 parts Silver Tequila
1 part Triple Sec
1 tsp. Fresh Lime Juice
1 Lime Twist

Combine liquid ingredients in a cocktail shaker with cracked ice. Shake well and strain into a chilled martini glass. Garnish with a lime twist.

Pomegranate Martini

1/2 cups Pomegranate Juice
2 oz. White Tequila
1 oz. Cointreau Liquor
Splash Sparkling Water
Squeeze Lemon
1 Pomegranate Fruit Slice

Combine liquid ingredients in a cocktail shaker with cracked ice. Shake and strain into a chilled martini glass. Garnish with a pomegranate fruit slice inside the drink.

Tequila Martini

2 1/2 oz. Jose Cuervo
   Tequila
1/2 oz. Dry Vermouth
1 Lemon Twist or Cocktail
   Olive

Combine liquid ingredients
in a cocktail shaker with
cracked ice. Shake well and
strain into a chilled martini
glass. Garnish with a lemon
twist or cocktail olive.

WHISKEY
&
BOURBON

MARTINIS

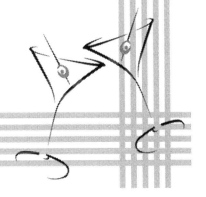

Alconquin Martini

1 1/2 oz. Whiskey
1 oz. Dry Vermouth
1 oz. Pineapple Juice
1 oz. Club Soda

Combine whiskey, vermouth and pineapple juice in a mixing glass with cracked ice. Stir to chill and strain into a chilled martini glass. Top with club soda and stir gently.

Black Rock Martini

1 1/2 oz. Jameson Irish Whiskey
1/2 oz. Blue Curacao
1/2 oz. Cognac
1 Maraschino Cherry

Combine liquid ingredients in a mixing glass with cracked ice. Shake and strain into a chilled martini glass. Garnish with a maraschino cherry.

Blue Monday Martini

2 oz. Whiskey
1/2 oz. Blueberry Brandy
1/2 oz. Fresh Sour Mix
1 Maraschino Cherry

Combine ingredients in a cocktail shaker with cracked ice. Shake and strain into a chilled martini glass. Garnish with a maraschino cherry.

Bourbon Chocolate Martini

1 1/2 oz. Bourbon
1/2 oz. Dark Creme de Cacao
1/2 oz. Godiva Liqueur

Combine ingredients in a mixing glass with cracked ice. Stir to chill and strain into a chilled martini glass.

Bourbon Cream Float Martini

2 oz. Bourbon
2 oz. Godiva Liqueur
1/2 oz. Heavy Cream

Combine bourbon and Godiva Liqueur in a mixing glass with cracked ice. Shake and strain into a chilled martini glass. Top with heavy cream.

Bourbon Kiss Martini

2 oz. Bourbon
1/2 oz. Dark Creme de Cacao
1/2 oz. White Creme de Cacao

Combine ingredients in a mixing glass with cracked ice. Stir to chill and strain into a chilled martini glass.

Bourbon Manhattan Martini

3 1/2 oz. Bourbon
1/2 oz. Dry Vermouth
1 Maraschino Cherry

Combine liquid ingredients in a cocktail shaker with cracked ice. Shake and strain into a chilled martini glass. Garnish with a maraschino cherry.

Bourbon Pie Martini

1 oz. Bourbon
1/2 oz. Dark Creme de Cacao
1/2 oz. Creme de Banane
1/2 oz. Milk

Combine ingredients in a mixing glass with cracked ice. Stir to chill and strain into a chilled martini glass.

Dirty Blonde Martini

2 oz. Vodka
1 oz. Johnnie Walker Gold
   Label
1 oz. Drambuie

Combine ingredients in a mixing glass with cracked ice. Stir to chill and strain into a chilled martini glass.

Dry Manhattan Martini

2 1/2 oz. Rye Whiskey
1/2 oz. Dry Vermouth
1 Lemon Twist

Combine liquid ingredients in a mixing glass with cracked ice. Shake and strain into a chilled martini glass. Garnish with a lemon twist.

Dubonnet Manhattan Martini

3 oz. Bourbon
1/2 oz. Dubonnet or
   Dubonnet Rouge
1/2 oz. Dry Vermouth

Combine ingredients in a cocktail shaker with cracked ice. Shake and strain into a chilled martini glass.

Equalizer Martini

2 oz. Bourbon
1/2 oz. White Creme de
   Menthe
3 dashes Grand Marnier

Combine ingredients in a cocktail shaker with cracked ice. Shake and strain into a chilled martini glass.

Four Seasons Manhattan Martini

2 1/2 oz. Rye Whiskey
1/2 oz. Sweet Vermouth
1 Maraschino Cherry

Combine liquid ingredients in a cocktail shaker with cracked ice. Shake and strain into a chilled martini glass. Garnish with a maraschino cherry.

Four Seasons Shamrock Martini

2 oz. Irish Whiskey
1 oz. Dry Vermouth
1 tsp. Green Creme de Menthe

Combine ingredients in a mixing glass with cracked ice. Stir to chill and strain into a chilled martini glass.

French Connection Martini

1 1/2 oz. Bourbon
1/2 oz. Pernod
1/2 oz. Dark Creme de Cacao
1 oz. Heavy Cream
Nutmeg

Combine liquid ingredients in a cocktail shaker with cracked ice. Shake and strain into a chilled martini glass. Sprinkle with nutmeg.

Hudson River Cocktail Martini

2 oz. Whiskey
1/2 oz. Dry Vermouth
1/2 oz. Orange Juice

Combine ingredients in a cocktail shaker with cracked ice. Shake and strain into a chilled martini glass.

Kentucky Martini

3 parts Kentucky Bourbon
1 part White Creme de
  Cacao
1 Maraschino Cherry

Combine liquid ingredients in a mixing glass with cracked ice. One part grenadine can be optionally added. Stir well and strain into a chilled martini glass. Garnish with a maraschino cherry.

Manhasset Martini

6 parts Rye Whiskey
1/2 part Dry Vermouth
1/2 part Sweet Vermouth
1 tbsp. Fresh Lemon Juice
1 Lemon Twist

Combine liquid ingredients in a cocktail shaker with cracked ice. Shake well and strain into a chilled martini glass. Garnish with a lemon twist.

Manhattan Martini

6 parts Rye Whiskey
2 parts Sweet Vermouth
1 dash Angostura Bitters
1 Maraschino Cherry

Combine liquid ingredients in a cocktail shaker with cracked ice. Shake well and strain into a chilled martini glass. Garnish with a maraschino cherry.

Mounted Cop Martini

2 oz. Whiskey
1/2 oz. White Creme de
  Cacao
1/2 oz. Heavy Cream
Nutmeg

Combine liquid ingredients in a cocktail shaker with cracked ice. Shake and strain into a chilled martini glass. Sprinkle with nutmeg.

Perfect Manhattan Martini

6 parts Rye Whiskey
1 part Dry Vermouth
1 part Sweet Vermouth
1 Maraschino Cherry

Combine liquid ingredients in a cocktail shaker with cracked ice. Shake well and strain into a chilled martini glass. Garnish with a maraschino cherry.

Scarlett Martini

1 1/2 oz. Southern Comfort
  Peach Liqueur
1 1/2 oz. Cranberry Juice
1 Lime Wedge

Combine ingredients in a cocktail shaker with cracked ice. Shake and strain into a chilled martini glass. Garnish with a lime wedge.

Southern Cream Pie Martini

2 1/2 oz. Bourbon
1 tsp. Superfine Sugar
1/2 oz. Light Cream
Nutmeg

Combine ingredients, except nutmeg, in a mixing glass with cracked ice. Shake and strain into a chilled martini glass. Sprinkle with nutmeg.

Statue of Liberty Martini

3 oz. Bourbon
1/2 oz. Cointreau
1/2 oz. Grenedine
1 Maraschino Cherry

Combine liquid ingredients in a cocktail shaker with cracked ice. Shake and strain into a chilled martini glass. Garnish with a maraschino cherry.

Sweet Manhattan Martini

2 1/2 oz. Rye Whiskey
1/4 oz. Sweet Vermouth
1/4 oz. Maraschino Liqueur
1 Maraschino Cherry

Combine liquid ingredients in a cocktail shaker with cracked ice. Shake and strain into a chilled martini glass. Garnish with a maraschino cherry.

Taxi Cab Martini

2 oz. Whiskey
2 oz. Orange Juice
1 tbsp. Lemon Juice
1 Lemon Twist

Combine liquid ingredients in a mixing glass with cracked ice. Stir to chill and strain into a chilled martini glass. Garnish with a lemon twist.

SCOTCH

MARTINIS

Beadlestone Martini

6 parts Scotch
3 parts Dry Vermouth

Combine ingredients in a mixing glass with cracked ice. Stir well and strain into a chilled martini glass.

Blushing Scot Martini

2 oz. Scotch
1 oz. Godiva White
  Chocolate Liqueur
1/2 oz. Light Cream
1/4 tsp. Grenadine

Combine ingredients in a mixing glass with cracked ice. Shake and strain into a chilled martini glass.

Cherry Rob Roy Martini

2 oz. Scotch
1/2 oz. Sweet Vermouth
1/2 oz. Stock Maraschino
  Liqueur
1 Maraschino Cherry

Combine liquid ingredients in a mixing glass. Stir to chill and strain into a chilled martini glass. Garnish with a maraschino cherry.

Dry Rob Roy Martini

3 oz. Scotch
1/2 tsp. Dry Vermouth
1 Lemon Twist

Combine liquid ingredients in a mixing glass with cracked ice. Stir to chill and strain into a chilled martini glass. Garnish with a lemon twist.

Fancy Scotch Martini

2 oz. Scotch
1/2 oz. Triple Sec
1/2 oz. Fresh Sour Mix
1 dash Bitters

Combine ingredients in a cocktail shaker with cracked ice. Shake and strain into a chilled martini glass.

Four Seasons Rob Roy Martini

3 oz. Scotch
1 tsp. Sweet Vermouth
1 dash Orange Bitters
1 Orange Twist
1 Maraschino Cherry

Wet the rim of a chilled martini glass with an orange twist. Combine liquid ingredients in a mixing glass with cracked ice. Stir to chill and strain into the martini glass. Garnish with a maraschino cherry.

Original Rob Roy Martini

2 1/2 oz. Scotch
1/2 oz. Sweet Vermouth
1 Maraschino Cherry

Combine liquid ingredients in a mixing glass with cracked ice. Stir well and strain into a chilled martini glass. Garnish with a maraschino cherry.

Perfect Rob Roy Martini

3 oz. Scotch
1 tsp. Sweet Vermouth
1 tsp. Dry Vermouth
1 Lemon Twist

Combine liquid ingredients in a mixing glass with cracked ice. Stir to chill and strain into a chilled martini glass. Garnish with a lemon twist.

Scotch Alexander Martini

1 oz. Dewars White Label
   Scotch
1 oz. White Creme de Cacao
1 oz. Heavy Cream
Nutmeg

Combine liquid ingredients
in a cocktail shaker with
cracked ice. Shake gently
and strain into a chilled
martini glass. Top with a
sprinkle or two of nutmeg.

Scotch Irish Shillelagh Martini

2 oz. Scotch
1/2 oz. Sloe Gin
1/2 oz. Light Rum
1/2 oz. Fresh Sour Mix
1 Maraschino Cherry

Combine liquid ingredients
in a cocktail shaker with
cracked ice. Shake and
strain into a chilled martini
glass. Garnish with a
maraschino cherry.

Scotch Blossom Martini

3 oz. Scotch
1/2 oz. Orange Liqueur
1/2 oz. Orange Juice
1 Orange Twist

Combine ingredients in a
mixing glass with cracked
ice. Stir well and strain into
a chilled martini glass.
Garnish with an orange
twist.

Scotch Milk Punch Martini

2 oz. Scotch
1 oz. Milk
1 tsp. Superfine Sugar
Nutmeg

Combine ingredients,
except nutmeg, into a
cocktail shaker with cracked
ice. Shake gently and strain
into a chilled martini glass.
Sprinkle with nutmeg.

Scotch On The Grill Martini

3 oz. Scotch
1/2 oz. Sweet Vermouth
3 dashes Angostura Bitters
1 Lemon Twist

Combine liquid ingredients in a mixing glass with cracked ice. Stir to chill and strain into a chilled martini glass. Garnish with a lemon twist.

Summer Scotch Cocktail Martini

2 oz. Scotch
1/2 oz. Dry Vermouth
2 oz. Grapefruit Juice
1 Lime Twist

Combine liquid ingredients in a mixing glass with cracked ice. Stir to chill and strain into a chilled martini glass. Garnish with a lime twist.

Tipperary Scotch Cocktail Martini

1 oz. Scotch
1 oz. Sweet Vermouth
1 oz. Green Chartreuse
1 Maraschino Cherry

Combine liquid ingredients in a mixing glass with cracked ice. Stir to chill and strain into a chilled martini glass. Garnish with a maraschino cherry.

OTHER

MARTINIS

Alize Martini

2 1/2 oz. Alize Liqueur
1 oz. Vodka

Combine ingredients in a mixing glass with cracked ice. Stir well and strain into a chilled martini glass.

Black Martini

2/3 oz. Gin
1/3 oz. Black Sambuca

Combine ingredients in a cocktail shaker with cracked ice. Shake gently and strain into a chilled martini glass.

Cherry Pie Martini

2 oz. Vodka
1 oz. Brandy
1 oz. Cherry Brandy

Combine ingredients in mixing glass with cracked ice. Stir to chill and strain into a chilled martini glass.

Chocolate Banana Martini

2 parts Vodka
1 part Creme de Cacao
1 part 99 Bananas (99 proof banana liqueur)
1 Hershey's Kiss

Combine liquid ingredients in a mixing glass with cracked ice. Stir well and strain into a chilled martini glass. Garnish with a Hershey's Kiss or Godiva Chocolate.

Danish Martini

6 parts Aquavit
1 part Dry Vermouth
1 Cocktail Olive

Combine liquid ingredients in a cocktail shaker with cracked ice. Shake well and strain into a chilled martini glass. Garnish with an olive.

Kojak Martini

2 oz. Vodka
1 oz. X-RATED Fusion Liqueur
1 drop Vermouth
few drops Lime Juice
1 Tootsie Pop lollypop (Cherry)

Combine vodka, vermouth and X-RATED Fusion Liqueur in a cocktail shaker with cracked ice. Shake well and strain into a chilled martini glass. Add a few drops of lime juice. Drop in a cherry Tootsie Pop upside down like Kojak use to eat. This is an original ShotDrinks.com cocktail.

Percolator Martini

1 oz. Vodka
1 oz. Cognac
1 oz. Grand Marnier
1 oz. White Creme de Cacao

Combine ingredients in a mixing glass with cracked ice. Stir to chill and strain into a chilled martini glass.

Pink Squirrel Martini

1 oz. Creme de Cacao
1 oz. Creme de Noyaux
1/2 oz. Skyy Vodka
1 oz. Heavy Cream

Combine ingredients in a cocktail shaker with cracked ice. Shake and strain into a chilled martini glass.

Princess Elizabeth Martini

6 parts Sweet Vermouth
1 part Dry Vermouth
2 tsp. Benedictine

Combine ingredients in a cocktail shaker with cracked ice. Shake well and strain into a chilled martini glass.

Silver Steak Martini

6 parts Gin
3 parts Jagermeister
1 Lemon Twist

Combine liquid ingredients in a cocktail shaker with cracked ice. Shake well and strain into a chilled martini glass. Garnish with a lemon twist.

Swiss Alps Martini

1 oz. Vodka
1 oz. Godiva White
   Chocolate Liqueur
1 oz. White Creme de Cacao
1 oz. Light Cream
Chocolate Shavings

Combine liquid ingredients in a mixing glass with cracked ice. Shake and strain into a chilled martini glass. Garnish with chocolate shavings.

Watermelon Martini

1/2 oz. Fresh Lemon Juice
1 oz. Midori Melon Liqueur
1 oz. Citrus Vodka
1 1/2 oz. Fresh Watermelon
   Juice
1 Mint Sprig

Combine liquid ingredients in a cocktail shaker with crushed ice. Shake gently and strain into a chilled martini glass. Garnish with a sprig of mint.

X-Rated Flirtini

1 part X-Rated Fusion
1 part X-Rated Vodka
1 Lemon Slice

Combine ingredients in a cocktail shaker with crushed ice. Shake gently and strain into a chilled martini glass. Garnish with a lemon slice.

INDEX

Made in the USA
Coppell, TX
11 December 2020